The Historical Jesus and the Kingdom of God

Present and Future
in the Message and Ministry of Jesus

Richard H. Hiers

University of Florida Press
Gainesville · 1973

Library of Congress Cataloging in Publication Data

Hiers, Richard H. 1932–
    The historical Jesus and the kingdom of God; present
and future in the message and ministry of Jesus.

    (University of Florida humanities monograph no. 38)
    Includes bibliographical references.
    1. Eschatology—Biblical teaching. 2. Jesus
Christ—Teachings. 3. Jesus Christ—Historicity.
I. Title. II. Series: Florida. University, Gaines-
ville. University of Florida monographs. Humanities, no. 38.
BS2417.E7H53   232.9'08   73–2623
ISBN 0–8130–0386–5

Preface

THIS IS A book that should be pleasing to few readers. It is meant for those interested in considering what can be known about the historical Jesus, both specialists in New Testament and nonspecialists. Specialists may be aggravated to find occasional commonplace or cursory reviews, e.g., such questions as the synoptic "sources," circumlocutions for the divine name, and the Son of man sayings. (The term "synoptic" refers to the first three Gospels, Matthew, Mark, and Luke. When "looked at together" they present much the same account of Jesus' activities and doings.) Nonspecialists may feel intimidated by the barrage of primary and secondary citations. Both specialists and nonspecialists are likely to be offended by the apparent irrelevancy of this study, or, worse yet, by what they may misconstrue to be its negative or even scandalous implications for theology and ethics.

In brief, the thesis argued here is this: Jesus believed that the Present world was about to end, in fact, that certain preliminary events marking the last days of the Old world had already begun to occur, and that the final and decisive events—the coming of the Son of man, the Judgment, and the Kingdom of God—would take place soon. Not only did Jesus so believe and proclaim; he also acted accordingly. Many of his actions that otherwise seem strange or incoherent are found to be entirely consistent with the structure of his beliefs and expectations.

I am well aware that this thesis will be disputed by many who have formed other opinions of the matter. In order to present the proposed interpretation clearly and objectively, priority has been given to primary sources, which are quoted and otherwise cited rather more frequently and abundantly than would be necessary if the thesis were less against the stream of popular and even scholarly understanding. If the argument seems to be a "tour de

iii

force," a piling up of evidence upon evidence, this is intended. In the process, several related discussions that might have been pursued further into the secondary literature have received little space.

The arrangement of the book into a series of short, systematic, and separate sections may appear somewhat artificial, since several of the topics are closely related to one another. But this seemed a better way to proceed than to take on everything at once. The reader is occasionally referred to exegetical and critical literature, but no strictly exegetical work is presented here. Though it is necessary often to note that certain traditions may represent the editorial or creative work of the Church, the main focus of the study is upon the historical Jesus: what he intended and what he did. Thus, the project is mainly historical and descriptive. If the results of the study are also thought by some readers to be significant for ethics and theology, I will not be displeased.

This study is, in a sense, a companion to my volume *The Kingdom of God in the Synoptic Tradition* (1970). There, I undertook a critical review of recurrent tendencies in the secondary literature and a series of exegetical studies of key and generally controverted passages. Here I attempt to set forth in positive terms the basic pattern of Jesus' ministry and message, especially as it may be understood with reference to his beliefs concerning the Kingdom of God, based on the conclusions of these and other critical and exegetical studies.

I should like to express my gratitude to my teachers in biblical studies, ethics, and theology: Richard T. Lyford, Kenneth R. Balsley, Paul W. Meyer, B. Davis Napier, Erich Dinkler, Marvin Pope, Millar Burrows, Liston Pope, James M. Gustafson, Roland Bainton, Robert L. Calhoun, and the late Kenneth Underwood, Paul Schubert, and H. Richard Niebuhr. I am indebted to each in many ways but certainly none is responsible for my errors in this study. I am particularly grateful also to Delton L. Scudder for several very helpful suggestions.

Biblical quotations from the Revised Standard Version of the Bible, copyrighted 1946 and 1952, by the Division of Christian Education of the National Council of Churches, are used by permission. I also thank the editors of the *Journal of Biblical Literature* for permission to reproduce here as sections 19 and 20 portions of the substance of two articles published in that journal, "Not the

Season for Figs" (1968) and "Purification of the Temple: Preparation for the Kingdom of God" (1971). Thanks go also to the Humanities Council and the Division of Sponsored Research of the University of Florida for research grants in connection with this project, and to the Graduate School of the University of Florida for making possible the publication of this monograph.

Richard H. Hiers

ABBREVIATIONS

BA	*Biblical Archeologist*
Billerbeck	H. L. Strack and P. Billerbeck, *Kommentar zum neuen Testament aus Talmud und Midrasch* (Munich, 1922–28), 4 vols.
JAAR	*Journal of the American Academy of Religion*
JBL	*Journal of Biblical Literature*
JR	*Journal of Religion*
JTS	*Journal of Theological Studies*
KGST	R. H. Hiers, *The Kingdom of God in the Synoptic Tradition* (Gainesville: University of Florida Press, 1970)
NT	*Novum Testamentum*
NTS	*New Testament Studies*
RSV	Revised Standard Version
SBT	Studies in Biblical Theology
SJT	*Scottish Journal of Theology*
TWNT	*Theologisches Wörterbuch zum neuen Testament,* ed. G. Kittel, 1932 ff.
ZNW	*Zeitschrift für die neutestamentliche Wissenschaft*

Contents

I

In Quest of the Historical Jesus

T HE LAST several years have witnessed an explosion of
scholarly literature concerned with what James M.
Robinson has termed a "new quest of the historical Jesus."[1] Actually, the quest for the historical Jesus has been going on for a long
time. Its earlier history is detailed most notably in Albert Schweitzer's volume written in 1906, which in English translation bears
the title *The Quest of the Historical Jesus*.[2] The exact relation between the earlier "quest" and the "new" is not altogether clear.
Robinson, for example, contrasts the new quest (and "new historiography") favorably with the "positivistic" interest of the old
in mere "brute facts." Yet Schweitzer (and more recently Rein-
hard Slenczka) established beyond doubt that the earlier quest
was characterized by subjectivity and dogmatic interest, not by
objectivity or "historicism."[3] Its proponents generally wished to
discover a historical Jesus whose intention, mission, and message
might lend credence to the gospel according to liberal Christianity
as against the doctrines of traditional orthodoxy. Proponents of the
"new quest," on the other hand, seem to be searching for a historical Jesus whose ideas and actions might be found more congenial to Bultmannian and "post-Bultmannian" conceptions of the
kerygma or "preaching" and doctrines of the Church about him.[4]

1. *A New Quest of the Historical Jesus*, SBT no. 25 (London: SCM Press,
1959). The discussion is usually said to have begun with Ernst Käsemann's
1953 lecture, "The Problem of the Historical Jesus," reprinted in his *Essays
on New Testament Themes*, SBT no. 41 (London: SCM, 1964), pp. 15–47.
2. See especially the third English edition with a new preface (1950) by
the author (London: Adam & Charles Black, 1954).
3. Robinson's allegation has been challenged, e.g., by Daniel L. Deegan,
"Albrecht Ritschl on the Historical Jesus," *SJT* 15 (1962):133–50. See Rein-
hard Slenczka, *Geschichtlichkeit und Personsein Jesu Christi* (Göttingen:
Vandenhoeck & Ruprecht, 1967).
4. See Leander E. Keck, "Bornkamm's *Jesus of Nazareth* Revisited," *JR*

2   THE HISTORICAL JESUS AND THE KINGDOM OF GOD

Schweitzer disclosed the irony that the supposedly undogmatic historical Jesus sought by the liberal proponents of the quest turned out to be an adherent of certain dogmas of first-century apocalyptic Judaism. The intention, mission, and message of the historical Jesus could be understood only in terms of the eschatological[5] beliefs which he shared with some of his Jewish predecessors and contemporaries, and his own special interpretation of these beliefs. The historical Jesus was the eschatological Jesus. Schweitzer's position is frequently misrepresented or distorted. It is assumed by many that Schweitzer concluded that the historical Jesus could not be found. Others assume that Schweitzer dismissed the historical Jesus as "deluded," a "fanatic."[6] But neither of these popular assumptions is correct. Schweitzer held that much could be said with a high degree of probability about Jesus' public ministry. Moreover, he did not regard Jesus as a "deluded fanatic," and decisively refuted the pathetic efforts of certain early twentieth-century psychopathologists to depict Jesus as a victim of paranoia or other psychosis. Nor is it the case, though it is often repeated as final truth, that Schweitzer considered the historical Jesus irrelevant for modern faith and life or declared that the his-

49 (1969):2–17. Elsewhere, Keck also criticizes the tendency of the "new hermeneutic" to conform Jesus to its ideological constructs, and its related inability to recognize the apocalyptic mode of his faith understanding (*A Future for the Historical Jesus* [Nashville: Abingdon Press, 1971], pp. 31, 262). As if to illustrate this point, Käsemann writes, " 'Does the history of Jesus—his words, works and suffering—already contain the kerygma in essence?' This must be so. . . . I am unable to understand Jesus as an apocalyptic figure . . . " (*New Testament Questions of Today* [Philadelphia: Fortress Press, 1969], pp. 50 f.). Käsemann is basically correct when he states elsewhere in the same book, "Neither the Anglo-Saxon nor the French-speaking lands have ever really come to terms with the question of the Jesus of history" (pp. 11–12). But this problem is not confined to scholarship in the lands mentioned.

5. The term "eschatology" here refers, inclusively, to teachings or doctrines concerning the events expected to occur near and at the end of the Present age and at the beginning of the Age to come.

6. Since these writers consider it self-evident that Jesus was not deluded or fanatical, this kind of characterization of Schweitzer's position seems to be an effort to discredit his analysis generally, and thus avoid having to deal with the evidence on which his interpretation rests. Generally, such writers wish to maintain that Jesus considered the Kingdom of God to be both present (in some sense) and future. For recognition of the latter truth, Schweitzer is generally commended. But then it is asserted, often, that Schweitzer's Jesus was "just a 'wild-eyed eschatologist,' " a "wild apocalyptic figure," or the like; e.g., John Reumann, *Jesus in the Church's Gospels* (Philadelphia: Fortress Press, 1968), p. 41; Käsemann, *New Testament Questions*, p. 42.

torical, eschatological Jesus could have no meaning for us today.[7] It is not claimed here that Schweitzer solved all aspects of the question of the historical Jesus. Schweitzer did not always carry through the eschatological interpretation with sufficient thoroughness. For instance, he did not explore the eschatological significance of Jesus' demon-exorcisms. Various features of his account of Jesus' purpose and activity remain questionable, for example, his proposal that Jesus intended to hasten the coming of the Kingdom through the repentance aroused by his (and his disciples') preaching, or his contention that Jesus deliberately provoked the Jewish authorities to bring about his suffering and death so that he, himself, might thereby bear the tribulations prerequisite to the coming of the Kingdom of God.

Nevertheless, both in his analysis of the earlier "lives of Jesus" and in his own studies of the historical Jesus, Schweitzer established beyond reasonable doubt the thesis earlier advanced by Johannes Weiss,[8] that Jesus thought and acted in accordance with certain Jewish eschatological beliefs understood in his own special way. Contrary to the pronouncements of apologists for various traditional or modern interests, subsequent findings with regard to then contemporary Judaism and early Christianity have strengthened the case for the kind of interpretation pioneered by Weiss and Schweitzer.

The principal problem about the quest for the historical Jesus is not whether it is possible, but rather that the historical Jesus

7. Even Robinson and Kee say that Schweitzer concluded that Jesus was a fanatic: Robinson, "Introduction" to *The Quest of the Historical Jesus* (New York: Macmillan, 1968), p. xiii; Howard Clark Kee, *Jesus in History* (New York: Harcourt, Brace & World, 1970), pp. 17–18. Schweitzer analyzed the psychiatric studies of Jesus in his M.D. dissertation (1913), *The Psychiatric Study of Jesus* (Boston: Beacon Press, 1948). Schweitzer's own position was set forth in 1901, in *The Mystery of the Kingdom of God* (New York: Macmillan, 1950), and again fifty years later in *The Kingdom of God and Primitive Christianity* (New York: Seabury Press, 1968). See also, especially, *Out of My Life and Thought* (New York: Henry Holt, 1949), chap. 6, and *Geschichte Der Leben-Jesu-Forschung* (Tübingen: J. C. B. Mohr [Paul Siebeck], 1951), pp. 631–42. For a review of Schweitzer's conception of Jesus and his significance, see R. H. Hiers, *Jesus and Ethics* (Philadelphia: Westminster, 1968), pp. 39–78.

8. *Die Predigt Jesu vom Reiche Gottes* (Göttingen: Vandenhoeck & Ruprecht, 1892), E. T. *Jesus' Proclamation of the Kingdom of God* (Philadelphia: Fortress Press, 1971). See also rev. ed., 1900. For a review of Weiss' significance, see David Larrimore Holland, "History, Theology, and the Kingdom of God," *Biblical Research* 13 (1968):1–13.

thought and acted in terms of a world view so different from our own as to render problematic his significance for contemporary Christian faith and ethics. Bultmann's demythologizing program was, in part at least, developed in response to this problem.[9] Much of the "new quest" literature, however, ignores or attempts to minimize the eschatological character of Jesus, as if somehow a noneschatological, historical Jesus might be discovered if only the right kind of methodology, hermeneutic, or historiography were employed. Discussions as to the "legitimacy" of the quest, a theological topic with which the "new quest" has been preoccupied, have no bearing upon the historical-descriptive task at hand.

Schweitzer used the term "thorough-going" or "consistent eschatology" to distinguish his own interpretation of Jesus' message and mission from those—notably, that of Johannes Weiss—which, in Schweitzer's judgment, explained Jesus' message by reference to his eschatological beliefs, but did not explain his mission or activity.[10] To varying degrees, the eschatological character of Jesus' preaching or message has come to be recognized in scholarly circles. Very little attention, however, has been given to the escha-

9. Rudolf Bultmann, *Jesus Christ and Mythology* (New York: Charles Scribner's Sons, 1958). Here it is primarily the thought and message *of Jesus* that Bultmann wishes to demythologize. Curiously, Bultmann wished to invoke Jesus' authority for ethics, but not for theology. Bultmann's demythologizing program, together with his effort to find the existential meaning both of Jesus' message and the kerygma of the early Church, have served to rehabilitate the New Testament for many Protestant American (especially southern) conservatives or "fundamentalists" who otherwise faced what seemed an irreconcilable choice between biblical faith and the world view of modern science. Similarly, C. H. Dodd's program of "realized eschatology" has functioned to rehabilitate Jesus and his message for British and American liberals (and Platonists) who preferred to believe that he had intended his ethical principles for people in all times to come. Both Bultmann and Dodd tend to attribute their own interpretations to Jesus himself. In their zeal to present Jesus as a modern moralist, they obscure and distort the evidence with respect to Jesus' intention and activity in his own time. The greatest achievement of Amos Wilder's *Eschatology and Ethics in the Teaching of Jesus* (New York: Harper, 1950) is that it succeeds, some of the time at least, in separating the historical-descriptive tasks from the theological-interpretive ones. Thus, Wilder can maintain correctly that Jesus looked for the coming of the Kingdom of God in the near future, and then go on to search for the basis of the continuing significance of his "ethics" in the "fundamental" sanctions, God's nature and will. Similarly, Harnack proposed to distinguish between the time-conditioned and the "essential" elements in Jesus' message. On the contributions and limitations of the proposals of Harnack, Bultmann, Dodd, and others, see Hiers, *Jesus and Ethics*.

10. Actually, Weiss also interpreted much of Jesus' activity in terms of eschatology, e.g., *Jesus' Proclamation*, pp. 74–80, 87–89.

tological character of his activity. Yet if Jesus thought, preached, and taught in accordance with a fairly definite pattern of eschatological beliefs, it would be strange if he did not also conduct himself accordingly. In fact, there is considerable evidence that he did act in accordance with his eschatological beliefs. His ministry both in Galilee and on the way to and in Jerusalem was entirely consistent with these beliefs, and is comprehensible only by reference to them.

Because it has been so largely neglected in the past, the greater part of this study (Chapters III and IV) will be devoted to an examination of the eschatological character of Jesus' activities, and of those sayings which occur in connection with such activities.

The term "eschatology" means a doctrine or conception of the end or the last times. When applied to the Jewish (and early Christian) notion of two ages, the Present age and the Age to come (or Messianic Age or Kingdom of God), its exact significance may be unclear. If one describes a certain phenomenon as "eschatological," is it meant that the phenomenon was expected to occur in the last days of the Present age or in the ultimate era, the Kingdom of God? The expression "latter" or "last days" may be similarly confusing. The term "realized eschatology" is likewise ambiguous. As generally used, for instance, by C. H. Dodd, it is meant to signify the presence of the Kingdom of God. Yet a number of eschatological phenomena, according to both Jewish and early Christian expectations, were understood to be preliminary and preparatory to the arrival of the Coming age or Kingdom of God, for instance, the return of Elijah and the outpouring of the spirit. In other words, certain eschatological phenomena might be "realized" or actualized in the present, but the coming of the Kingdom of God would remain for the future.

The synoptic evidence leaves little doubt that Jesus expected the coming of the Kingdom of God, the Son of man, the time of Judgment, and also, probably, the resurrection of the dead of previous generations, to take place in the future, in fact, in the near future.[11] The Present age or world would give way to a New world: the

---

11. In addition to Weiss and Schweitzer, such diverse and significant scholars as O. Betz, R. Bultmann, M. Burrows, H. J. Cadbury, M. Dibelius, M. S. Enslin, R. M. Grant, E. Grässer, D. J. Selby, K. Stendahl, M. Werner, and H. Windisch concur in this judgment. Cf. Wolfhart Pannenberg, *Theology and the Kingdom of God* (Philadelphia: Westminster, 1969), esp. pp. 51–55.

Kingdom of God would then be established both in heaven and on earth.

It is also clear, though not so generally recognized, that Jesus interpreted a number of present phenomena, including his own activity and that of his followers, as decisive eschatological occurrences, preliminary to these future events and, in one way and another, preparatory for them. Jesus' evident understanding of and participation in these preliminary eschatological phenomena will be the subject of the third chapter of this study.

Several features of Jesus' activity on the way to and in Jerusalem also seem related, in various ways, to Jewish eschatological doctrines. Undoubtedly many details were supplied by early Christian writers following certain supposedly prophetic or christological biblical texts.[12] Yet one cannot preclude the possibility that Jesus himself acted in accordance with his own understanding of certain prophecies and expectations.[13] Many of the sayings and actions attributed to him both in Galilee and on the way to and in Jerusalem indicate a definite eschatological, if not also messianic, self-understanding. That this is the case with respect to one or another of these sayings or actions has been recognized by the writers of many articles, monographs, and commentaries. But, to date, the basic pattern common to these several units of tradition has not been presented as a whole.

---

12. E.g., the description of soldiers casting lots for Jesus' garments (Mark 15:24 and parallels), and the Johannine invention of the "seamless robe" (John 19:23 f.) in order to fulfill literally Ps. 22:18 which speaks both of dividing up garments and of casting lots; the Johannine additions about the soldiers' piercing Jesus' side and breaking the legs of the others (John 19:31–37; cf. Zech. 12:10, Exod. 12:46); and Matthew's story about the thirty pieces of silver (Matt. 27:3 ff.; cf. Zech. 11:12 f.). The Matthean version of the fate of Judas and the naming of the Field of Blood seems to depend on both the Syriac and the Hebrew readings of Zech. 11:13! Typically, Matthew conflates the two, working both "treasury" and "potter" into his account. Cf. Acts 1:18 ff., which has recourse to an entirely different tradition and "prophecy" (Ps. 69:25). This psalm also may supply the detail that "they" gave him vinegar to drink (Mark 15:36; cf. Ps. 69:21b). That such details had to be supplied from Scripture, imagination, or hearsay is not surprising: upon Jesus' arrest, his followers "all forsook him and fled" (Mark 14:50). On this general subject, see also Morton S. Enslin, *The Prophet from Nazareth* (New York: McGraw Hill, 1961), pp. 156–57, and Keck, *A Future*, pp. 108, 140–41nn30–31.

13. Thus also David E. Aune, "The Problem of the Messianic Secret," *NT* 11 (1969):22 ff. Especially important in this connection are Isa. 52–53, Zech. 1–14, and the book of *Enoch*.

A word is in order about the sources for the study of the historical Jesus. It is widely recognized that the few nonbiblical or "secular" allusions to Jesus in other historical records tell little or nothing about him.[14] The Dead Sea Scrolls (despite the inventive genius of certain of their interpreters) tell nothing about the historical Jesus, though they do provide a wealth of additional information on the period in which he lived.[15] There may be at least echoes of Jesus' sayings in some of the Nag-Hammadi writings, e.g., the *Gospel of Thomas*, but their principal value lies in what they tell us about the situation and beliefs of the Gnostic-Christian communities in which they were composed.[16] The historical value of the Gospel according to John is approximately of the same order. It is a theological treatise on the significance of Jesus and the importance of believing in him, written in the form of an account of his sayings and doings. That this is the case may still be shocking to laymen, but it has been known, if not always acknowledged, by critical New Testament scholars for the last ninety years. The apostle Paul occasionally seems to cite from a tradition containing some of Jesus' sayings, sometimes referring to matters which he has from "the Lord," but in some of these instances, he may have meant special private revelations instead (e.g., I Cor. 7:10, 12, 25; II Cor. 12:1 ff.).

Virtually the only sources for a study of the historical Jesus are the first three Gospels, Matthew, Mark, and Luke. But none of these, with the possible exception of Mark, was written by anyone who had known or seen Jesus. They report earlier recollections of what Jesus did and said, but these recollections and reports of the tradition were unquestionably shaped at many points by the life

14. For brief summaries of evidence given by Josephus, Tacitus, Suetonius, and Pliny the Younger, see Martin Dibelius, *Jesus* (Philadelphia: Westminster Press, 1949), pp. 17–19; Otto Betz, *What Do We Know About Jesus?* (Philadelphia: Westminster Press, 1968); Robert A. Spivey and D. Moody Smith, Jr., *Anatomy of the New Testament* (New York: Macmillan, 1969), pp. 172–73.

15. See Miller Burrows, *More Light on the Dead Sea Scrolls* (New York: Viking Press, 1958), esp. pp. 38–132, and Betz, *What Do We Know?*, passim.

16. See Robert M. Grant and David Noel Freedman, *The Secret Sayings of Jesus* (London: Collins Press, 1960), p. 16: "[The Gospel of Thomas] is probably our most significant witness to the early perversion of Christianity by those who wanted to create Jesus in their own image. . . . Ultimately it testifies not to what Jesus said, but to what men wished he had said." See also Günther Bornkamm, in Bornkamm, Hahn, and Lohff, *What Can We Know About Jesus?* (Philadelphia: Fortress Press, 1969), p. 74.

situations, needs, and developing doctrines of the early churches, and also, probably, by the religious, literary, and other interests of their evangelist–editors. No single unit of tradition ("pericope") can be proven to be an exact account of what Jesus said or did. The evidence may have some cumulative weight, but one cannot speak with absolute certainty.

Probably Mark's Gospel was the earliest written, for both Matthew and Luke apparently utilized his narrative framework and much of his material, though not without some alterations.[17] There are also traditions, mainly sayings, that appear in both Matthew and Luke, but not in Mark. Presumably such traditions were not taken by Matthew and Luke from Mark or Mark's sources, but from some other "source," either oral or written. This hypothetical source is generally designated "Q" for *Quelle*, a German word meaning "source." It may be, however, that "Q" is also represented by some of the sayings that appear only in Matthew or only in Luke, which, for some reason, were omitted by the other evangelist. Thus, although it may be that traditions which appear in Mark or "Q" come from an earlier and possibly more reliable layer of tradition than those found only in Matthew or only in Luke, not even this is certain.

Where the problems or concerns of the later church seem to be reflected in a particular tradition, one may plausibly suspect that it has been altered, as in the case of Matthew's additions to Mark 1:9; 10:11 f., and his revisions of Mark 10:17 f., 21.[18] Other criteria for differentiating between more and less probably authentic traditions are discussed in the last section of this study.

The gospels do not give the kind of information one would need in order to write a complete "life of Jesus." The birth and infancy stories are mainly legendary in character. We do not know in which year, or even which decade, Jesus was born or died. If the story of the wise men, the star, and Herod (Matt. 2) could be considered historically accurate, it would imply a date before 4 BC, since Herod died in that year. Thus Jesus could have been born as

17. The reader who wishes to follow the argument closely might well have at hand a copy of *Gospel Parallels*, ed. Burton H. Throckmorton, Jr. (Camden: Thomas Nelson & Sons, 1967), and perhaps also a critical edition of Greek text. The priority of the Markan version of a given pericope cannot always be assumed, even if W. R. Farmer has not yet proven the priority of Matthew.

18. Cf. Matt. 3:14 f.; 5:32 = 19:9; 19:16 f., 21.

early as 6 BC. The Lukan narrative, however, dates Jesus' birth at the time of "the first enrollment, when Quirinius was governor of Syria" (Luke 2:2). This would suggest the year 6 AD. That Jesus was executed sometime between 26 and 36 AD is probable, since Pontius Pilate was procurator during these years. Luke tells that Jesus was "about thirty years of age" at the beginning of his ministry (3:23), but in John's gospel, "the Jews" (who in this gospel are generally made to speak their malevolent lines in unison) note that Jesus is "not yet fifty years old" (8:57). Despite innumerable pious and impious speculations as to his activities during his "silent years," we know virtually nothing about him until the beginning of his ministry as an adult. And we do not know much about his adult ministry—at most, what the evangelists tell us, which does not even include an indication as to the length of his public career. Was it but a few weeks, or did it span a number of years?

All things considered, the term "historical Jesus" in the title would be pretentious and erroneous if it were intended that the writer thought that he was about to present the life and thought of Jesus, or even of his adult ministry, as it actually happened. The sources simply are not such as to allow one to say without further ado, "Here is what he said, and here is what he did." What is meant by the title is that the study focuses on the historical Jesus. Looking at the evidence as objectively as one can, and weighing it in terms of probabilities, what was his message, what did he do, and what did he evidently mean by what he said and did?

Not only Christian interpreters but non- and anti-Christian writers have tended to think of Jesus in accordance with their own doctrines and values, in order to vindicate their own viewpoints and traditions. People will tend to understand any question, initially at least, to the degree that it fits into their own previous perceptions and commitments. How much more so has this been true in the question of the historical Jesus! In this study, I am not concerned with the immediate relevance of my findings. Too many studies have been vitiated by the quest for relevance. The greater the urge for relevance, the stronger the temptation to bend the evidence to suit one's theology or theory as to what is relevant.[19] Here, within the limits of the evidence and probability,

19. I have examined this problem in *Jesus and Ethics*, esp. pp. 115–39, and "The Historical Jesus and the Historians," *Dialog* 11 (1972):95–100. John

the concern is to try to determine what may have been Jesus' own understanding of his message and mission, not what we would like it to have been. Having said this, I will admit to the convictions that what is true is ultimately relevant, and that what is true about the historical Jesus can only lead to a better understanding of his relevance for faith and life.

Reumann and Martin Hengel provide an excellent critique of recent efforts to claim Jesus as a fellow revolutionary in Hengel, *Was Jesus a Revolutionist?* (Philadelphia: Fortress Press, 1971).

II

Jesus' Message, Beliefs, and Expectations

SEVERAL excellent books have been written on the subject of Jesus' message and beliefs, including, for instance, extensive discussions of the parables, of his "ethical" (and other) "teaching," and the meaning of the "Son of man" in the sayings attributed to him. Many of these studies are still useful. In recent years, however, attention has turned for the most part from the message and beliefs of Jesus to the history of the oral and literary traditions, especially sayings attributed to him ("form criticism"), the beliefs of Paul and other Christians about him ("the kerygma"), and the interests and editorial work of the evangelists who compiled—if not composed—the traditions ("redaction criticism").

Usually a writer's theological interests tend to leave their mark on his account of Jesus' message and beliefs. Liberal writers, for example Wendt and Harnack, discovered in Jesus the great Teacher who founded the tenets of Protestant liberalism. The "new quest" writers were and are inclined to present the historical Jesus as the original proponent of one or another special version of Bultmann's somewhat existentialist, but also somewhat Lutheran, understanding of the so-called kerygma. Nearly all writers on the subject have desired to be both objective and relevant to their own times. This has not been an easy assignment, however. What has often happened is that objectivity has had to make room for relevance.

The central feature of Jesus' message and expectation, viewed with historical objectivity, has been subjected to all kinds of devious and ingenious interpretation by diverse theological scholars, primarily, it seems, because it has appeared as an otherwise insurmountable obstacle to the relevance of Jesus and his teaching for faith and ethics. (The liberal writers were more interested in

11

the relevance for ethics, the "new quest," and older conservative writers more in the relevance for faith.) This feature is his proclamation and expectation that the Kingdom of God was near. Because so many "relevant" but historically and exegetically questionable ideas about the Kingdom of God have been read into the message of Jesus, many people today are confused as to the meaning of this expectation as Jesus understood it.[1] My effort here will be to try to establish what the Kingdom of God, together with related beliefs and expectations, meant for the historical Jesus. The evidence is not always conclusive, and often one must be content with only possibilities. But the basic pattern is fairly certain. Because Jesus' thought world (and that of then contemporary Judaism and early Christianity) is so strange to us, the primary evidence will be introduced in abundance. This approach seems necessary if the doctrines and outlooks of later times are to be penetrated.

When the nature of Jesus' beliefs and declarations becomes clear, it may then be possible to venture to describe the ways in which his "ministry"—his activity as a whole—was grounded in and carried out in accordance with the beliefs and expectations.

The coming of the Kingdom of God was not the only thing Jesus proclaimed or expected. A whole series of events and actions are closely correlated: the coming time of tribulation, the resurrection of the dead of previous generations, the appearance of the Son of man and the Great Judgment before this Son of man's throne, entrance into the final state of blessedness for those who will be invited to "inherit" the Kingdom, and the final consignment of the wicked to Gehenna. In the meantime, Jesus called on his hearers (and those to whom he sent the twelve missionary–disciples) to trust in God and do His will: to be ready for the events to come.

1. THE NEARNESS OF THE KINGDOM OF GOD AND THE CERTAINTY OF ITS COMING

Jesus did not undertake to convince his Jewish contemporaries that the era of salvation for which they had been longing—some

1. See my article "Eschatology and Methodology," *JBL* 85 (1966):170–84 (=*KGST*, pp. 6–21), and the introduction by D. Larrimore Holland and myself to Johannes Weiss, *Jesus' Proclamation of the Kingdom of God* (Philadelphia: Fortress Press, 1971), pp. 2–53.

of them, at least—was about to begin. He simply announced that
the Kingdom of God had come near. Such, in essence, was his
message, as summarized by the first two evangelists (Mark 1:15=
Matt. 4:17). John the Baptist had said exactly the same thing, according to Matthew (3:2). It was to proclaim this good news that
Jesus subsequently sent his followers hurrying through the northern
Jewish towns: "Repent, the Kingdom of God has come near."[2]

Several passages state simply that Jesus preached the gospel of
the Kingdom of God (Matt. 4:23; 9:35) or taught about it (Luke
9:2, 11), without saying explicitly that he looked for this great
event in the near future. According to Luke 4:43, Jesus understood
his mission to be primarily to preach the good news of the Kingdom of God to the Galilean (or all Jewish?) cities of his day.
Since he puts it explicitly on so many other occasions,[3] Luke probably thought it unnecessary to specify at every opportunity that
the good news consisted of the announcement and expectancy
that this still future era of salvation would—sooner or somewhat
later—assuredly come to be.

At any rate, there is ample evidence in the first three Gospels to
support the conclusion that Jesus looked for and proclaimed the
coming of the Kingdom of God as the decisive and future occur-
rence to be reckoned with by his hearers.

He taught his followers that they should pray for its coming:
"Thy Kingdom come!" (Matt. 6:10=Luke 11:2). The obvious implication is that the Kingdom of God had not yet come. The petition does not ask for the final "consummation" of a Kingdom which
had, somehow or other, already come, or that men might come to
realize had already come, or that its presence might be experienced
still more profoundly—interpretations actually advanced by recent
interpreters. Jesus meant his disciples to pray that God would
cause His Kingdom to *come,* to be established on earth. Elsewhere
he had urged them to desire it above all else, and assured them
that God would hear their prayers and give the Kingdom to them
(Matt. 6:33; Luke 12:31 f.; 18:1-8).

That at least some of his hearers would live to see the coming
of the Kingdom is stated clearly in Mark 9:1: "Truly, I say to you,

2. Matt. 10:7=Luke 10:9, 11. Kingdom of heaven, a term used frequently
by Matthew, is equivalent to Kingdom of God. "Heaven" here is a circumlocution, a way of avoiding use of the divine name.
3. E.g., Luke 10:9, 11; 11:2; 19:11; 21:31; 22:16, 18.

there are some standing here who will not taste death before they see the Kingdom of God come with power." The saying appears as the final assurance and warning that "life" (in the Kingdom of God) is worth infinitely more than possessions, even possession of the whole world of the Present age, and that the fate of each person will be decided on the basis of his present responsiveness to Jesus and his words when the Son of man comes in the glory of his Father—at the dawning of the Kingdom of God. The coming of the Kingdom of God and that of the Son of man are described in much the same terms. Mark 9:1 refers to the coming of the Kingdom of God "with power," a phrase used in Mark 13:26 with respect to the manner of the coming of the Son of man. Matt. 16:28 (cf. Mark 9:1) speaks of the coming of the Son of man instead of the Kingdom of God, while Luke 21:31 reads Kingdom of God in place of the Son of man (Mark 13:29). Elsewhere, also, the two are closely or interrelated (e.g., Luke 17:20—18:8). The coming of the Kingdom of God was to be a world-shaking event. The power and glory of God would be universally and vividly manifested on that day (Mark 13:24–26 and parallels). It may be that the words "*some* standing here" (Mark 9:1 and parallels) and "this generation" (13:30 and parallels) were later added to the tradition in order to extend the hope that the promise would be fulfilled to those living at a somewhat later time in the first century.[4] But it is as clear as can be that Jesus meant his hearers to understand that the promise and warning about the coming of the Kingdom of God and Son of man were to be fulfilled in the future.

The expectation of the Kingdom of God was not confined to the early period of Jesus' ministry. At the Last Supper with his disciples, he vows that he will abstain from drinking wine until the day when he shall drink the new wine that will grace table in the Kingdom of God, or, as Luke puts it, "until the Kingdom of God comes" (Mark 14:25 = Luke 22:18). He tells the High Priest and those with him that they will see the coming of the Son of man enthroned at the right hand of Power.[5] After his execution, a certain Joseph of Arimathea (whom Matthew describes as a disciple of Jesus) was still "expecting" (*prosdechomenos*) the Kingdom of

4. See sec. 27 of this study.
5. "Power" here is another circumlocution for God. Perhaps this is the basis for the expression "in" or "with power" in Mark 9:1 and 13:26: God himself is to be manifested at the time of the coming of the Son of man. Cf. Dan. 7:9–13.

God (Mark 15:43). The inference that the Kingdom of God had not yet come is sufficiently obvious.

Certain other terms are also used to designate the era or status of blessedness characterized by the Kingdom of God. The "Age to come" or "Coming age"—a term common in Jewish sources—is mentioned several times, always as a future era, as indicated both in the structure of the expression itself and in its various contexts (e.g., at Mark 10:30 and Matt. 12:32).[6] "Eternal life" or simply "life" is also used in this sense. In the Age to come, those who are found worthy will inherit, receive, and enjoy eternal life (Mark 10:17, 30, and parallels). In the account of the rich man who wished to know how he might inherit "eternal life," it is clear that the terms "eternal life" and "the Kingdom of God" are used interchangeably (cf. 10:23–26). "Life" in the Kingdom of God or Age to come is what those will "find" who "lose" their life—their worldly goods and projects—because of their fidelity to Jesus and his words.[7] The gate is narrow and the way hard that leads to life— eternal life in the Kingdom of God (Matt. 7:14). To "enter life" is to "enter the Kingdom of God" (Mark 9:43, 47).

In the "beatitudes" Jesus pronounces blessed those who now suffer humiliation, hardship, and persecution, for they shall have satisfaction and all-surpassing joy in the Kingdom of God (Luke 6:20–23). The Matthean version, which may also reflect authentic traditions, includes as blessed the meek, the merciful, the pure in heart, the peacemakers, and those who seek righteousness, for they shall inherit the earth, i.e., the Kingdom of God when it is established on earth. Here they will obtain mercy, they shall see God, they shall be called sons of God. It is understandable that Luke sums this all up in the declaration which he attributes to Jesus: "Then [when the Son of man comes] your redemption is drawing near" (21:28).

Jesus was certain that the Kingdom of God would come soon, at the latest while some of those about him were still alive. In all

6. Mention of the still future "Age to come" at Matt. 12:32 proves what might not otherwise be so clear, that Matthew understood the saying about the Kingdom of God in 12:28 as a reference to its future, perhaps even imminent, coming, rather than its presence. See *KGST*, pp. 30–35. Although the contrary is sometimes asserted, there is no reason to doubt that, in the synoptic tradition, "Kingdom of God" and "Age to come" are equivalent terms. See Enslin, *Prophet*, p. 71.

7. Mark 8:35–37 = Matt. 16:25 f. = Luke 9:24 f.; Matt. 10:38 f. = Luke 17:33; cf. John 12:25.

likelihood, he proclaimed its imminence: it was coming very soon, it could come at any time. For this reason, numerous sayings and parables emphasize the need for constant readiness: "Watch! For you do not know the day or the hour."[8]

Certain of the parables have suggested to some interpreters that Jesus thought of the Kingdom as already present on earth, perhaps in connection with himself or his activity, and growing or developing toward its fulfillment, in particular the parables of the seed growing secretly, the mustard seed, and the leaven (Mark 4:26–29, 30–32; Matt. 13:33 = Luke 13:20 f.). Each begins with the formula "The Kingdom of God is as if [or "like"]. . . ." Each *could* mean that the Kingdom, like seed in the ground or leaven in a batch of dough, was already here, though invisible or inconspicuous, growing toward a visible manifestation. The point of comparison would then be growth. However, it is equally possible and more consistent with the evidence which looks to the coming of the Kingdom as a still future event, to see the point of comparison in the certainty with which the final result may be expected. Those who know that seed has been sown or dough leavened—in short, who know what is happening—may anticipate the harvest or rising of the dough with confidence.[9] Such parables would have meaning only if one accepted the "mystery" or "secret" (Mark 4:11) which was at the same time the thematic public proclamation of Jesus, that the Kingdom of God was really coming. To those who had ears to hear (4:22 f.), Jesus and his message were the sign of the times.[10]

2. THE "ETHICAL" PREACHING AND TEACHING OF JESUS

The all-surpassing importance of the Kingdom of God.—Jesus announced the nearness of the Kingdom and called on his hearers to

8. Mark 13:33–37; Matt. 24:42; 25:13; Luke 12:38, 40, etc.

9. Thus, e.g., Enslin, *Prophet,* pp. 73–74. The idea of harvest and the expectation of preternatural growth and fertility in the Age to come are common motifs in Jewish literature of the period. See my article "Not the Season for Figs," *JBL* 87 (1968):395–97. In regard to the parable of the mustard seed, see esp. Ezek. 17:22–24.

10. Cf. Matt. 16:1–4; Luke 12:54–56; see especially secs. 10 and 12 of this study.

repent (Mark 1:15=Matt. 4:17). Jesus, and before him John, had appeared in the role of Jonah, the preacher of repentance to the men of Nineveh.[11] Numerous sayings and parables stress the importance of repentance: the sayings about the Galileans executed by Pilate and the victims of the tower that fell in Siloam ("unless you repent you will all likewise perish" [Luke 13:1–5]); the exclamations about Chorazin, Bethsaida, and Capernaum,[12] and about the Queen of the South and the men of Nineveh (Matt. 12:39–42= Luke 11:29–32); the two sons (Matt. 21:28–32); the lost sheep (Matt. 18:10–14=Luke 15:4–7); the lost coin and the prodigal son (Luke 15:8–32). Jesus sent the Twelve through the towns of Galilee not only to proclaim the nearness of the Kingdom of God, but to preach that men should repent (Mark 6:12).

The basic meaning of the verb "to repent" (*shūb*) is to "turn." Jesus summoned his hearers to turn from all else to God, to abandon everything and everyone that could keep them from seeking "first"—above all else—the Kingdom of God (Matt. 6:33= Luke 12:31). The Kingdom could be entered only by the narrow gate and the path that is hard (Matt. 7:13 f.=Luke 13:23 f.). Such was the choice which Jesus called upon his hearers to make, God or possessions:[13] "For whoever would save his life will lose it, and whoever loses his life for my sake will find it. For what will it profit a man if he gains the whole world and forfeits his life?" (Matt. 16:25 f.=Luke 9:24 f.). Ultimately it was a choice between having one's life in the Present age or having life in the Age to come.

Perhaps Jesus meant his saying about cutting off the offending hand, foot, or eye only figuratively, to dramatize the central idea, as in his saying about the camel going through the eye of a needle or the piece of timber in one's brother's eye. But there is no doubt that he meant the warning with the utmost seriousness: "It is better for you to enter [the Kingdom of God] with one eye, than with two eyes to be thrown into Gehenna" (Mark 9:43–47; cf. Matt. 18:8 f.). And it may be that Matthew elaborated this theme, understanding it to imply not only a caution against marriage, but also the advisability of literal self-castration: "There are eunuchs who have

11. See sec. 12 of this study.
12. Matt. 11:20–23 = Luke 10:13–15.
13. Matt. 6:24 = Luke 16:13; Mark 10:17–30 = Matt. 19:16–29 = Luke 18:18–30.

made themselves eunuchs for the sake of the Kingdom of heaven. He who is able to receive this, let him receive it" (Matt. 19:12).

There is little reason to doubt, however, that Jesus himself called on those who would inherit the Kingdom to forsake not only those to whom they had legal and moral obligations but those whom they most loved. A would-be follower wished to bury his father. But Jesus ordered, "Follow me, and leave the dead to bury their own dead" (Matt. 8:21 f. = Luke 9:59 f.). Another wanted to say farewell to those at home. "No one who puts his hand to the plow and looks back is fit for the Kingdom of God." The "sword" that Jesus said he came to bring was one of division within families— one must choose between loved ones and the way to the Kingdom:

> For I have come to set a man against his father,
>   and a daughter against her mother. . . .[14]
> There is no man who has left house or wife
>   or brothers or parents or children
> For the sake of the Kingdom of God
>   who will not receive . . . in the Age to come eternal life.[15]

These harsh sayings, generally ignored by those who write about "Jesus and the family," can only be understood when one recognizes the urgency of the times.[16] It was a matter of life and death. One could not have it both ways. This was the situation: The Kingdom of God was coming. Would people be ready for it, willing to sacrifice all for the sake of gaining entrance into the Kingdom? One must "sit down and count the cost" (Luke 14:28–32; cf. 12:57–59). But the cost is everything one has: "So therefore whoever of you does not renounce all that he has cannot be my

14. Matt. 10:34–37 = Luke 12:51–53; 14:26. Cf. *Enoch* 100:2.

15. Luke 18:29b–30; cf. Matt. 19:29; Mark 10:29 f. It may be that the words "manifold more *in this time*" are authentic, and referred to the blessings of companionship—with their true relatives, those who do the will of God (Mark 3:32–35; cf. Luke 11:27 f.)—which Jesus' followers would enjoy together with him *before* the beginning of the Age to come. Or this idea may represent the experience of the church awaiting the parousia later in the first century. Mark 10:30 particularly seems to represent such experience.

16. William E. Phipps illustrates the aberrations that may arise from ignoring the eschatological context of Jesus' mission and message: "Why, then did Jesus call attention to those extreme situations when severing close ties with natural affections becomes mandatory? Probably his own personal struggle with family pressures caused this emphasis" (*Was Jesus Married?* [New York: Harper & Row, 1970], p. 77).

disciple" (Luke 14:33; cf. 12:33). He who seeks to save his life in this world will lose it in the Age to come. The Kingdom of God is like the treasure hidden in a field, the pearl of value beyond all pearls, for the sake of which one joyfully sells all that he has (Matt. 13:44–46). Repentance, renunciation: here is what one must do! Turn from all the treasures and ties of one's life in this world to God and the great chance for eternal life in the Kingdom of God.

Faith and ethics for the interim.—The "ethics" of Jesus was "interim ethics," ethics for the interim, a summons to action in the time that remained before it was too late, before the coming of the Kingdom and the time of Judgment.[17] The coming of the Kingdom and Judgment marked the end of the period in which Jesus called on his hearers to respond. Afterwards, it would be too late. To some degree, as noted in connection with the "harsh" sayings, the urgency of the times also shaped the content of the response to which he summoned them: a radical choice between the Kingdom of God and all else they held dear. As Weiss put it, "He summons them, therefore, to the frightful challenge, like the physician who confronts his patient with the choice between a perilous operation or letting things take their course. A half remedy will not do."[18] But the imminence of the Kingdom did not entirely determine the character of the response to which he called them. The imminence of the Judgment did not occasion an interim (or teleological) suspension of the ethical. Rather, it was all the more important that people now trust God and do his will.[19]

Matthew reports a series of sayings on trusting and serving God and Him only, which he presents, appropriately, between Jesus' instructions about praying for the coming of the Kingdom of God and his concluding sayings about doing the will of God as the way to enter it when it does come (6:10—7:21 ff.). The sayings about practicing piety (6:1–18) and those about anxiety (6:25–34) also fit well in this context: those who really trust God give alms, pray to Him, and fast without needing to be esteemed by their fellow

17. See my article "Interim Ethics," in *Theology and Life* 9 (1966):220–33, and my book *Jesus and Ethics*, pp. 91–93, 134–37.

18. *Jesus' Proclamation*, p. 111; see also pp. 105–14.

19. Cf. H. Richard Niebuhr, *Christ and Culture* (New York: Harper, 1951), pp. 15–29.

men. Those who really trust God have no need to be anxious about food, drink, clothes, or life—especially if God's Kingdom is coming soon. Jesus summoned his hearers to have confidence that God would hear their prayers and give them what they longed for, the Kingdom of God.[20]

In numerous places, generally in connection with an exorcism or healing, Jesus calls for and responds to faith, confidence in God's ability to bring about the desired deliverance. Sometimes it is the faith of those who desire him to heal someone else, as in the case of the paralytic (Mark 2:5 and parallels), Jairus' daughter (Mark 5:36 = Luke 8:50), the Syrophoenician woman's daughter (Mark 7:29 = Matt. 15:28), or the centurian's slave (Matt. 8:10 = Luke 7:9). Or it may be the person to be healed (or exorcised) whose faith is said to be the basis for the healing: the woman with the hemorrhage (Mark 5:34 and parallels), and Bartimaeus (Mark 10:52 = Luke 18:42). In other situations also, Jesus calls on his followers to trust God to care for them, in the storm at sea (Mark 4:40), or under any circumstances.[21]

His hearers were to believe the good news (= "gospel") that the Kingdom was coming, and trust God to care for them in the meantime. Only those who did so believe would find it possible to give up all else for the sake of the eternal life that was promised them in the Age to come.

Believing in God, trusting in Him above all else, was also necessary for doing his will: "You cannot serve God and mammon" (Matt. 6:24 = Luke 16:13), mammon, of course, meaning wealth, possessions. Several sayings and parables stress the importance of doing God's will. It is not enough simply to profess fidelity: "Not everyone who says to me, 'Lord, Lord,' shall enter the Kingdom of heaven, but he who does the will of my Father who is in heaven."[22] It is the will of God that Jesus proclaims to his hearers as that which they are to do, emphasized by the comparison of the two houses (or foundations) that concludes the Sermon on the Mount: "Everyone who hears these words of mine and does them will be like a wise man who built his house upon the rock . . . " (Matt. 7:24–27 = Luke 6:47–49). Those who do the will of God

20. Matt. 7:7–11 = Luke 11:9–13; Matt. 6:25–33 = Luke 12:22–32; Luke 18:1–8.
21. Mark 9:23; Matt. 17:20 = Luke 17:6; Mark 11:22–24 = Matt. 21: 21 f.
22. Matt. 7:21 ff.; cf. 25:31–46; Luke 6:46.

are the ones Jesus acknowledges as his true kinsmen.[23] Seeking the Kingdom of God and doing His will are more important than bonds of family. The two, in fact, are the same: to seek the Kingdom of God means to do His will.

What is the will of God? Jesus seems to have understood that the "Law of Moses," the Torah, was still the basic guide for his fellow Jews. A rich man wanted to know what he must do to inherit the Kingdom of God. Jesus directed his attention to the Ten Commandments (Mark 10:17–30 and parallels). He declared that not the smallest part of any letter of the Law would go out of effect while the Present age continued (Matt. 5:18=Luke 16:17). But the will of God was not contained or confined in the Law; it was much more far reaching and radical.

Jesus may even have subscribed to the interpretations of the Pharisees: "Practice and observe whatever they tell you," he advised his followers, according to Matt. 23:3. But their interpretations of the will of God were not radical enough: "Unless your righteousness exceeds that of the scribes and Pharisees, you will never enter the Kingdom of heaven" (Matt. 5:20). It was not enough to refrain from killing; one must refrain from anger and insult and seek reconciliation (5:21–24). It was not enough to refrain from technical adultery; one must refrain from looking lustfully at a married woman (5:27 f.). Moses had permitted divorce "because of your hardness of heart"; but the intention of God, revealed in the biblical story of creation, was that there should be no divorce, because if people divorce and remarry, they commit adultery against their former spouses (Mark 10:7–12). It was not enough to refrain from making false promises or testimony in the name of God; one should not swear by any of the substitutes or circumlocutions for God's name either (Matt. 5:33–37). Though the Law permitted it, one should not return evil for evil, or do merely what one has to when importuned, but one should give more than is asked for. It is not enough to love one's neighbor while hating one's enemy; those who would be "sons of their Father" should also love their enemies, as God himself blesses both the righteous and the unrighteous (5:43–48; cf. 5:9). Love and justice were the "weightier matters of the Law," even if the other matters were not to be neglected (Matt. 23:23=Luke 11:42).

23. Mark 3:33 f. = Matt. 12:49 f. = Luke 8:21; Luke 11:27 f.

Implicitly, Jesus seems to have understood that what God willed was, essentially, the well-being of life, especially human life. Keeping the law was less important than responding helpfully to human needs and feelings. The honor due to father and mother—financial support in their old age—was not to be withheld on the grounds that it had been pledged to the Temple (Mark 7:10–13). Anger was bad not only because it might lead to killing, but because it injures a person's sense of worth and relationships between persons. Divorce is bad not only because it contradicts the divine intention but because it is harmful to the welfare and sensitivities of the one against whom it is committed. The Sabbath was made for man, not man for the Sabbath. The Law was for the good of the Jewish community: what God wills, both in and beyond His Law, is what is good for man.[24] So the disciples may "work" by breaking off ears of grain, even though it is the Sabbath, for they are hungry, just as David and his companions, when they were in need of food, had eaten the sacred bread that was reserved by law for the priests. So those who are sick or possessed by demons are to be healed on the Sabbath, even though strict constructionists might view this as a violation of the law against working on the Sabbath (Luke 13:10–17). It is lawful to do good, both to man and beast, on the Sabbath, even if it means doing some work.[25] Jesus commended as fit for the Kingdom of God the scribe who declared the commandments to love God with all one's capacity and love one's neighbor as one's self more important than all the burnt offerings and sacrifices prescribed by the Law (Mark 12:32–34; cf. Matt. 22:37–40 = Luke 10:27).

Love of God meant trusting Him and preferring His Kingdom above all other would-be masters, treasures, and ties. It also meant devotion to his will, and what He wills means doing that which is good for other persons, responsiveness to others as persons having worth in the eyes of God and as worthy of love. "Whatever you wish that men would do to you, do so to them; for this is the law and the prophets" (Matt. 7:12 = Luke 6:31).

The description of the Great Judgment in Matthew 25 underscores responsiveness to those in need as the essence of what God wills. Those who will be invited to inherit the Kingdom are those

24. Mark 2:27 f.; cf. Deut. 10:12 f. See Weiss, *Jesus' Proclamation*, pp. 124–26.
25. Mark 3:1–5 = Matt. 12:9–13 = Luke 6:6–10; Luke 14:1–6.

who gave food to the hungry, drink to the thirsty, welcome to the stranger, clothing to the naked, and time and assistance to the sick and the imprisoned. Those, on the other hand, who would be sentenced to the eternal fire of Gehenna had not done anything wicked. They had simply been unconcerned about those they might have helped. The same point is made in the parable of the Good Samaritan (Luke 10:25–37). The Samaritan responded to the injured traveler with the kind of care he would have desired had he been in that situation. He treated him as a person whose well-being was a matter of importance, with some time, trouble, and a little money. Perhaps Jesus meant his hearers to understand that the priest and Levite who passed by on the other side of the road had wished to preserve their ritual cleanliness. In any case, they had done nothing against the Law; they simply had not been helpful to a man in need. This was the notable failing also of the rich man who had feasted sumptuously every day while Lazarus lay sick and hungry at his gate.

Perhaps, in Jesus' view, the danger of wealth—for those who wished to inherit the Kingdom—was not only that it might come before God in one's devotion, but that those who keep it for themselves in a hungry and needy world necessarily do so by neglecting those they might have helped. There can be no question that he understood and urged that wealth should be used for the poor. "Go, sell what you have, and give to the poor, and you will have treasure in heaven" (Mark 10:21 = Matt. 19:21 = Luke 18:22). "How hard it will be for those who have riches to enter the Kingdom of God!"[26] A camel can go more easily through the eye of a needle than a rich man through the narrow gate that leads to the Kingdom of God. The poor, on the other hand, would inherit the Kingdom of God (Luke 6:20 f.; 14:15–24; 16:22). The poor would be in a position to receive others into the eternal habitations: it was not only loving and right, but also prudent to befriend the poor in this world by means of unrighteous mammon.[27] "Sell your possessions, and give to the poor; provide yourselves with purses that do not grow old, with a treasure in heaven that does not fail. . . " (Luke 12:33; cf. Matt. 6:19 f.). "When you give a feast,

26. Mark 10:23 = Matt. 19:23 = Luke 18:24; cf. Luke 6:24 f. See Enslin, *Prophet*, pp. 98–110.
27. Luke 16:1–9; James 2:5; see my article "Friends by Unrighteous Mammon," *JAAR* 38 (1970):30–36.

invite the poor, the maimed, the lame, the blind, and you will be
blessed, because they cannot repay you. You will be repaid at the
resurrection of the righteous" (Luke 14:13 f.). It was not always a
matter of wealth. But it was always a matter of responsiveness to
those in need. Even something as simple as a cup of water given
to a thirsty child was important and a mark of a true disciple; one
who did such a thing would not lose his reward, the hoped-for
blessedness of life in the Kingdom of God (Matt. 10:42).

Nor was it, essentially, a matter of giving things to others, but
rather of one's attitude toward others. Knowing oneself to be in
need of God's forgiveness, one ought not withhold forgiveness from
others.[28] Such a person should refrain from judging others ad-
versely, lest he be judged by the same standard (Matt. 7:1–5=
Luke 6:37 f., 41 f.). Such a person will reserve honor for others
(Luke 14:7–11); those who humble themselves now will be exalted then, when the Kingdom of God comes (Matt. 5:3, 5).
Those who aspire to greatness of life, if not also to ruling in the
Kingdom of God, must now become servants of all (Mark 9:33–35;
10:43 f.). If one will not live as a servant (*pais*) in preparation for
the Kingdom, he shall not enter it (Mark 10:15).

None of this was arbitrary or odd or immoral, as is claimed by
interpreters who are worried about the idea of "interim ethics" or
"rewards." The Judgment was near. Only those could enter who
had shown themselves fit recipients of life in the Kingdom of God,
by loving God above all else, and being concerned with their
neighbors in the same ways that they were concerned for themselves. The Kingdom would be given to "those producing the fruits
of it" (Matt. 21:43). The good tree bears good fruit; the good man
brings forth good (Matt. 12:33, 35=Luke 6:43–45), a point that
had been made earlier by John the Baptizer.[29]

3. THE COMING TRIBULATION

Jesus apparently shared the belief of certain of his Jewish predecessors and contemporaries that there would be a period of ter-

28. Matt. 6:12; 6:14 = Mark 11:25; Matt. 18:21 f. = Luke 17:3 f.;
Matt. 18:23–35.
29. Matt. 3:8–10 = Luke 3:8–9; cf. Luke 13:6–9.

rible "tribulation" or "temptation" before the final age of salvation could begin. The idea is represented in the Book of Daniel, for instance, by the vision of the terrible "fourth beast" and its war against the people of God, after which they will receive and possess the Kingdom for ever and ever (Dan. 7:7–27), and again in the visions and expectations of a final cosmic struggle between the power of God and that of Satan in Revelation and the Qumran War Scroll. The Evil One would then make his last effort to keep control over the kingdoms of the earth—a control which perhaps he had been given for a while by God,[30] or perhaps had usurped. If the time of tribulation was not part of the divine intention, it was, however, known by God, and part of the necessary scheme of history, for it had been revealed to the men of old.[31] Such ideas are attributed to Jesus in the so-called synoptic Apocalypse (Mark 13:5–37 = Matt. 24:4–42 = Luke 21:8–36). There would be wars and rumors of wars, nation rising against nation, earthquakes, and famines as just the beginning of the sufferings or "birthpangs" (ōdin, 13:8) of the Coming age;[32] then more persecutions, and the exhortation that "he who endures to the end" (of the tribulation) will be saved (13:13); then "the desolating sacrilege," flight, and "such tribulation [thlipsis] as has not been from the beginning of the creation which God created until now, and never will be" (sc., again, 13:19), followed by the appearance of false messiahs and prophets. Then, after that tribulation (13:24), the sun and moon will be darkened, the stars will fall from the heavens, and the powers (dunameis—the Satanic rulers, principalities?) in heaven will be shaken, and then—at last—the Son of man will be seen coming (13:26 ff.). It is very likely that the schematic arrangement of these phenomena (first this, then that, then that) is a creation of the early church.[33] But it is not so certain that the

30. Cf. Luke 4:5 f.; Job 1–2. See sec. 13 of this study.
31. In addition to the visions of Daniel, see also those of Joel (2:30—3:15); Zech. (11–14); IV Ezra, e.g., ch. 16; Baruch 27, 70; Enoch 90–100.
32. Cf. C. E. B. Cranfield, The Gospel According to Saint Mark (Cambridge: At the University Press, 1959), p. 397: "The Rabbinic expression 'the birth-pangs of the Messiah' (meaning not the sufferings of the Messiah but the sufferings expected to precede his coming) was probably already current in the time of Jesus. . . . The origin of the expression is perhaps to be seen in such passages as Isa. 26:17; 66:8; Jer. 22:23; Hos. 13:13; Mic. 4:9 f."
33. Note the evangelist's parenthetical word to "the reader" (13:14); see sec. 27 of this study.

idea of some kind of coming tribulation was foreign to Jesus' own expectation.

It appears prominently in the prayer he taught his disciples—not only as a model of brevity, but of substance. They were to pray not only that God would cause His Kingdom to come, but that He would not lead them into temptation (*peirasmos*, Matt. 6:13=Luke 11:4). In effect, Jesus taught them to pray that God might cause the Kingdom to come without permitting the scripturally appointed time of tribulation to take place first, that the tribulation might be omitted from the pattern of final events. The Matthean report or expansion "but deliver us from the Evil One" (6:13b) has exactly the same meaning: the tribulation was thought of as the last effort of Satan to subvert the faithful and keep his power on earth. Jesus' prayer in the garden, in which he urged his companions to join, was to the same effect, that the cup (of anticipated suffering) might pass from him (Mark 14:35, 36), that they might all be spared the necessity of the temptation (*peirasmos*).[34] Earlier he had told two of his companions that they would indeed share his "cup" and "baptism" (Mark. 10:39).

Jesus did not, in all probability, describe the "tribulation" in the detail provided in the "synoptic apocalypse." Much of the picture here comes from the traditional apocalyptic imagery that was familiar to the church in such places as Daniel, Joel, and possibly IV Ezra. Jesus did not, it seems, revel in the prospect of the cataclysm. But evidently he did believe that it must take place, unless, that is, God might choose to overrule the earlier revelations of what was to occur. It is a mark of Jesus' confidence in the power and goodness of God that he prayed and taught his followers to pray that God might, after all, spare them the necessity of going through temptation.

---

34. Mark 14:38 = Matt. 26:41 = Luke 22:46. Cf. Schweitzer, *Kingdom of God*, pp. 115–30. Thus also Reumann, *Jesus*, p. 105: "The term . . . used [in the Lord's Prayer] is one that in the writings of the day referred to trials of the last times (Mark 14:38), *the* Test, the final great trial—the danger of falling away from God. Matthew means us to see this sense when he adds, 'Deliver us from the Evil One.'" It is not certain, however, that this clause (Matt. 6:13b) should be considered a Matthean addition. It may have been part of the original saying. Elsewhere Jesus seems to have utilized the parallelism of form and imagery characteristic of Hebraic poetry (e.g., Matt. 6:24; 7:6; 10:34). The "Evil One," of course, is Satan. Thus also William Manson, *Jesus and the Christian* (Grand Rapids: Eerdmans, 1967), p. 83.

4. The Resurrection of the Dead

Jesus did not proclaim the resurrection of the dead to his contemporaries. It apparently was not a matter of great importance either to him or his hearers. At first, this fact may seem surprising.

One time (Mark 12:18–27 and parallels), some Sadducees, who apparently understood that Jesus did expect the dead to be raised, asked him a "trick" question about a woman who had married seven brothers, one after the other, each of whom had died, after which the woman herself died. "In the resurrection, whose wife will she be? For the seven had her as wife." Jesus' questioners assumed that everyone would agree that monogamy was the normative form of marriage, both in this life and "in the resurrection" (i.e., in the Coming age), though it is not prescribed in the Torah. Jesus did not bring up the subject of resurrection, but his answer implies that he shared the Pharisees' belief that the dead would be raised at the end of the Present age—at least, those who were to share the life of the Age to come. He referred to the scriptural tradition that God had declared himself to Moses as the God of Abraham, Isaac, and Jacob—all of whom, had, of course, died— and evidently understood this to mean that these three patriarchs would indeed be raised from the dead. Elsewhere he declares that Abraham, Isaac, and Jacob would sit at table in the Kingdom of God.[35]

Jesus did not offer his contemporaries the hope that they would be raised from the dead. The reason for this seems clear. The Kingdom of God had come near. His hearers would still be alive at the time of the Judgment, so they would not need to be raised from the dead! "Truly, I say to you all this will come upon this generation" (Matt. 23:36 = Luke 11:51). "Truly, I say to you, this generation will not pass away before all these things take place" (Mark 13:30 = Matt. 24:34–36 = Luke 21:32).

Consequently, when Jesus does speak of the resurrection of the dead, it is always the dead of previous generations who are to be raised. They are to be raised so that they can be judged with this generation, for the Judgment of all men has yet to take place (cf.

---

35. Matt. 8:11 = Luke 13:28 f. It is possible, however, that Jesus meant that these three patriarchs had, like Elijah, been transported (upon death) directly to heaven. In Luke 16:19–31, "Father Abraham" is already pictured in heaven or paradise, although the resurrection has not yet occurred.

John 5:28 f.). It will take place while the generation of Jesus' contemporaries are still alive:

> The men of Nineveh will arise at the judgment with this generation and condemn it;
> for they repented at the preaching of Jonah, and behold, something greater than Jonah is here.
> The Queen of the South will arise at the judgment with this generation and condemn it;
> for she came from the ends of the earth to hear the wisdom of Solomon, and behold, something greater than Solomon is here.[36]

In various traditions, Jesus speaks of the necessity of his own impending death and resurrection (Mark 8:31; 9:31; 10:33 f. and parallels; cf. 9:9 f.). The authenticity of these "predictions of the passion" has been disputed, and the general tendency of critical scholarship is to regard them as "prophecy after the fact," added by the church in order to legitimate the fact that Jesus had been executed, and to confirm belief in his resurrection. But, as we shall see, it is not unlikely that Jesus came to consider it possible or perhaps necessary that he would die, and that his death would prepare both for the coming of the Kingdom of God and his own future role as Son of man.[37] That he also may have expected to be raised from the dead is equally well attested and equally plausible, for the resurrection of the dead and the Judgment were to occur at the dawning of the Kingdom of God. If he, himself, expected to die and then be raised from the dead, his resurrection would be as the "first fruits of those who have fallen asleep" (I Cor. 15:20), the beginning of the "general" resurrection and Judgment.[38]

5. THE JUDGMENT BEFORE THE SON OF MAN

It is not certain that Jesus identified himself with the "Son of man" who was to preside at the Judgment. But unless one wishes

36. Matt. 12:41 f. = Luke 11:31 f.; see also Matt. 10:15 = Luke 10:12; Matt. 11:24; and Matt. 11:22 = Luke 10:14.
37. See secs. 8, 24–26 of this study.
38. Thus also Wolfhart Pannenberg, *Jesus—God and Man* (Philadelphia: Westminster Press, 1968), pp. 106–8.

to assign a substantial portion of the synoptic tradition to the inventiveness of the early church, it is quite probable that Jesus did expect and proclaim that someone was soon to appear as the Son of man, and that this one would be enthroned as Judge (if not also "King") over all men and nations, those of this generation and the risen dead of those that preceded.

The Judgment would occur after the end of the Present age with the coming of the Kingdom of God. Those who were to enter the Kingdom of God would first have to "stand before the Son of man" (Luke 21:36). It is not surprising that the two events, the coming of the Kingdom of God and the coming of the Son of man, are often interrelated or spoken of interchangeably (e.g., Mark 9:1 = Matt. 16:28; Mark 13:29 = Luke 21:31). In effect, both occur at the same time, as different aspects of the same great event. Both were expected to come soon, at any time. Mark 8:38 speaks of the coming of the Son of man, but the next verse of the Kingdom of God. In Matt. 10:7, Jesus instructs the Twelve to proclaim to the towns of Israel that the Kingdom of heaven is at hand, but concludes by telling them that they will not have completed their mission through the towns of Israel before the Son of man comes (10:23).[39] The saying at Luke 17:20 f. refers to the impending appearance of the Kingdom of God, an event that will be unmistakable and universally visible; the verses following (17:22—18:8) comprise several sayings pointing to the universally visible future and unmistakable appearance of the Son of man.[40]

Expectancy of the imminent appearance (or "parousia") of the Son of man is also evidenced in the several parables and sayings in which Jesus urged his disciples and hearers to "watch," to be in a constant state of preparedness, "for you do not know when the time will come."[41] Such also is the implication of his admonition, "Make friends quickly with your accuser, while you are going with him to court . . . " which is surely a piece of "ethics for the

39. See *KGST*, pp. 66–71.

40. Cf. Mark 13:24–27 and parallels; Matt. 24:26–28; and especially Luke 21:35: "For it will come upon all who dwell upon the face of the whole earth." Luke quotes (at 3:6) the salvation oracle of Isa. 40:5: "The glory of the Lord shall be revealed, and all flesh shall see it together." See my article "Why Will They Not Say, 'Lo, here!' or 'There!'?" *JAAR* 35 (1967):379–84 (= *KGST*, pp. 22–29).

41. Mark 13:33–37; also Matt. 24:42–44 = Luke 12:39 f.; Matt. 25:1–13; Matt. 24:37–41 = Luke 17:26 f., 34 f.; Matt. 24:45–51 = Luke 12:42–46; Luke 12:35–38; Mark 14:38 = Matt. 26:41. See *KGST*, pp. 72–77.

interim" and was not intended as a moral maxim for his followers in centuries to come.[42] Jesus assures his followers that their vindication, the coming of the Kingdom of God and the Son of man, will occur "speedily." The decisive question is, when the Son of man comes, will he find faith on earth, will men be doing the will of God? (Luke 18:8, 21:34–36). And he warned the High Priest and his other accusers that they, themselves, would see his vindication, "the Son of man sitting at the right hand of Power, and coming with the clouds of heaven" (Mark 14:62 = Matt. 26:64). Similarly, he advises his followers that they ("you," plural, again) would live to see his appearance (Mark 13:29 = Matt. 24:33).[43]

Apparently Jesus expected that the Twelve would also take part in the Great Judgment: according to the saying at Matt. 19:28 = Luke 22:29 f., their task, specifically, would be to judge the twelve tribes of Israel. Perhaps this is why Jesus had chosen twelve disciples in the first place: "Truly, I say to you, in the New world, when the Son of man shall sit on his glorious throne, you who have followed me will also sit on twelve thrones, judging the twelve tribes of Israel" (cf. I Cor. 6:2 f.). Who would enjoy the places of highest honor, sitting at the right hand and the left, was another matter. Those seats were reserved "for those for whom it has been prepared" (Mark 10:35–44 = Matt. 20:20–27). But Jesus advises those who aspire for greatness (as rulers?) in the Coming age that they must prepare for it by now being servant or slave (Mark 10:41–44 and parallels).

A few stylistic variations appear in the ideas about the Judgment. In Matthew, Jesus speaks of the angels of the Son of man who will accompany him at the time of Judgment (Matt. 13:41; 16:27; 24:31). Elsewhere angels are mentioned (Mark 8:38 = Luke 9:26) in connection with the Judgment, but they are not described as belonging to the Son of man. The idea is similar in each case: they are the attendants of the Son of man, and assist in the court proceedings as bailiffs, so to speak. In both Matthew and Luke, Jesus speaks of his Kingdom, or the Kingdom of the Son of man, in

42. Matt. 5:25 f. = Luke 12:57–59; cf. Luke 16:9: "Make friends for yourselves by means of unrighteous mammon. . . ."
43. It may be that the use of the third person plural ("they") in Mark 13:26 and parallels represents an attempt on the part of the editors of the tradition to extend the hope to those now living after the death of at least some in the original generation. Cf. Mark 13:30 and parallels, and see sec. 27 of this study.

each case referring to the time and place of the Judgment,[44] and twice in Matthew the Son of man is also referred to as "the King" (Matt. 25:34, 40). In Matt. 13:41–43, the idea seems to be that those who are approved by the Son of man from among those assembled for Judgment will then enter the Kingdom of God. The "Kingdom" of the Son of man, is, in effect, the courtroom where the Judgment is to take place. After the Judgment is over, the Son of man, presumably along with the righteous, would enter the Kingdom of God. There would no longer be a "Kingdom of the Son of man" (cf. I Cor. 15:24–28).

In Matthew's Gospel, Jesus uses the term "the Consummation" or "Close of the age" five times.[45] In three of them, the reference is clearly to the time of Judgment, and in all cases the meaning is implicitly the end of the Present age. The "Close of the age" is the time when the Kingdom of God will be established, and the Son of man will come to judge all mankind. Afterwards begins the Age to come, when all would enter the places of their respective final destinies.

6. The Blessings of Life in the Kingdom of God and the Fate of Those Excluded from It

Jesus did not attempt a description of the conditions of life in the Coming age. Some of the apocalyptic writers had done so, e.g., Ezekiel's vision of the ideal Temple (Ezek. 40–48), and such expectations as are represented in Amos 9:13–15, IV Ezra 2:10–48, *Jubilees* 23:26–31, *Enoch* 90:28–42, and *II Baruch* 29, 73–74 (cf. Isa. 11:6–9). Perhaps Jesus assumed that some of these images and ideas were familiar to his hearers. He did not repudiate them, but he did not repeat them either.

The transformation of the earth.—Several sayings suggest that he believed, as certain of the prophetic and apocalyptic writers had before him, that the present cosmos—both heaven and earth— would "pass away," and be replaced by a "new heaven and a new

44. Matt. 13:41; 16:28; 20:21; Luke 22:30; 23:42.
45. Matt. 13:39, 40, 49; 24:3; 28:20.

earth."[46] The anticipated darkening of the sun and moon, falling of the stars, and shaking of the "powers in the heavens" (planets, "principalities"—angelic or satanic?) are perhaps part of this picture (Mark 13:24 f.). The Temple buildings would be overthrown with the breakup of the Old world—perhaps to make way for a new Temple.[47] Jesus came, he said, to cast fire upon the earth, and longed for the time that it would be kindled (Luke 12:49 f.). The coming of the Son of man will be sudden and universally catastrophic—for the unrighteous, at any rate—as in "the days of Noah" or "on the day when Lot went out from Sodom" (Matt. 24:37–41 = Luke 17:26 f.; Luke 17:28–30; 21:34 f.).

A significant term is used for the "New world" in Matt. 19:28: *hē palingenesia*, literally "the new birth" or "regeneration." The term *ōdin*, meaning "birth pang" or "travail-pain," appears in the plural at Mark 13:8 = Matt. 24:8 with reference to the beginning of the "sufferings" or "tribulations" that must precede the coming of the Son of man and the era of final salvation. The idea seems to be that a radical transformation of the world must occur in the course of the emergence of the Kingdom of God on earth. This idea may be related to the expected tribulation which Jesus urged his followers to pray that God might spare them: Bring thy Kingdom, but lead us not into *peirasmos* (Matt. 6:10, 13 = Luke 11:2, 4). The Old world, ruled as it was by Satan and his demons, a place of hunger, sorrow, and affliction, would have to be radically changed before it could become the place where God ruled over his Kingdom.[48]

After this transformation (and the Judgment), "the righteous will shine like the sun in the Kingdom of their Father" (Matt. 13:43).[49] We do not know whether Jesus shared Paul's belief that those who entered the Coming age would first be "transformed," given a "spiritual body" (I Cor. 15:50–54; Phil. 3:21). A saying is attributed to him which may have a similar sense:

Truly, I say to you,
    unless you turn and become like children,
you will never enter the Kingdom of heaven (Matt. 18:3).

46. Matt. 5:18; Mark 13:31 = Matt. 24:35 = Luke 21:33; cf. Isa. 65:17; 66:22; *Enoch* 45:4 f.
47. Mark 13:1–4 and parallels; see sec. 22 of this study.
48. See Zech. 14:4–11; *Asmp. M.* 10:1–9.
49. Thus also *Enoch* 104:1–4.

This may, simply, be a Matthean variation on the saying in Mark 10:15 about making one's self ready to receive the Kingdom of God by becoming a servant or slave. But it might instead be related to a saying preserved in two forms in the Fourth Gospel—the only saying in that gospel about the Kingdom of God:

Truly, truly, I say to you unless one is born anew, he cannot see the Kingdom of God.	Truly, truly, I say to you unless one is born of the Spirit, he cannot enter the Kingdom of God.[50]

Here the individual is summoned to a radical transformation. The idea of transformation by the Spirit (of God) or "rebirth" suggests more than the spiritual and moral renewal implicit in the idea of repentance. A physical rebirth or transformation seems to be indicated.

John the Baptist, Jesus said, was the greatest of those born of women. But neither he nor anyone else born only of woman had yet entered the Kingdom of God. The implication seems to be that when the Kingdom comes, those who are to enter it would in some way need to be born again before they could enter it.[51] Jesus does not say so explicitly, but his response to the Sadducees who asked him about the future marital status of the seven brothers implies that not only the risen dead but those who are alive when the New age comes will be "like angels in heaven," neither marrying nor giving in marriage (Mark 12:25 = Matt. 22:30; cf. Luke 20:34–36). We are not told that Jesus had said, as Paul did, that "flesh and blood cannot inherit the Kingdom of God" (I Cor. 15:50). But Jesus may have expected that those who were to inherit eternal life in the transformed conditions of being in the Coming age would themselves be transformed, to some extent.

The most radically different aspect of the conditions of life in the New age would be that then God would rule the earth rather than Satan, the Caesars and Herods, the powerful and the rich. That first shall be last and the last first is the great refrain of warn-

50. John 3:3, 5. The reference to water in 3:5 seems to be an interpolation added in the interest of a later theory about baptism as necessary for salvation (cf. I Pet. 3:20 f.; I John 5:6–8). Jesus says nothing elsewhere in any of the Gospels about baptism as a prerequisite to entering the Kingdom of God.
51. Matt. 11:11 = Luke 7:28. See *KGST*, pp. 57–65.

ing and solace throughout the message of Jesus.[52] The poor, the meek, the hungry, the lowly, the disinherited in this life would then inherit the earth, the Kingdom of God established on a transformed earth (Matt. 5:3 ff.; Luke 6:20 f.). Then, when the Kingdom of God comes, God's will shall be done on earth, as it is already by the angels in heaven.[53]

Marriage.—There would be no marrying or giving in marriage in the Kingdom of God; men and women would be "like the angels" (Mark 12:25). Luke may have taken this to mean that those who longed for entrance into "that age" should therefore refrain from marriage, for they would not die before entering it, and thus might find themselves still married in a world where there was to be no marriage (20:34–36). Paul, who also expected to live until the coming of New age (I Thes. 4:15–17; I Cor. 15:51 f.), did not marry, and advised the unmarried to remain in that condition. This advice was given not because of the problem of having a wife in the New world but because of the impending tribulation[54] associated with the dissolution of the present form or shape of the Present age or "world" inasmuch as "the appointed time has grown very short" (I Cor. 7:25–31). Paul notes that he lacks any "command of the Lord" in regard to this question, which may mean that he did not know of any saying of Jesus on the subject. Matthew may have taken such sayings more literally, and attributed to Jesus the approbation of those who had made themselves eunuchs in order to prepare themselves for the Kingdom of God (19:12). However, in this context (19:3–11), such a radical strategy seems more intended to avoid the peril of adultery in the Present age than to transform oneself for the way of life appropriate to the Age to come. Probably Jesus had said nothing about the advisability or inadvisability of marriage in the remaining days of the Old world. But he had said that in the Kingdom of God there would be no marriage; people would live "like the angels."

52. Mark 10:31 = Matt. 19:30 = Luke 13:30; Matt. 20:16; Luke 14:11. So also Cranfield, *St. Mark*, pp. 323–24, on Mark 10:14: "The Kingdom of God belongs to little children—and to other weak and insignificant ones—not because of any merit of theirs but because God has willed to give it to them (cf. Luke 12:32)."

53. Matt. 6:10; cf. Jer. 31:31–34; 32:38–40; Ezek. 36:26–28.

54. I Cor. 7:26. Paul's term for "tribulation" here is *anankē*. See also Luke 21:23.

Eating and drinking in the Kingdom of God.—The life of those in the Kingdom would not be that of disembodied spirits.[55] One of the recurrent images in Jesus' sayings about life in the Kingdom is the banquet table, where the righteous will be gathered from the ends of the earth and heaven[56] and seated with fathers Abraham, Isaac, and Jacob: "I tell you, many will come from east and west, and sit at table with Abraham, Isaac and Jacob in the Kingdom of heaven."[57] At the Last Supper, Jesus looked forward to the time when, in the Kingdom of God, he would next drink of the fruit of the vine *in* the Kingdom of God.[58]

The prayer for the coming of the Kingdom had as a parallel expression the petition "Give us this day our bread for tomorrow" (Matt. 6:11). It was expected that bread would be on the banquet table in the Age to come (Luke 14:15; 22:16). The prayer asks that God would bring the bread of the Coming age, in effect, the Kingdom of God, this day, now.[59] Perhaps what Paul intended at Rom. 14:17 was that the Kingdom of God meant not only food and drink, but also righteousness and peace and joy in the Holy Spirit. Jesus apparently understood and intended his hearers to understand that it would mean, among other things, food and drink; those who now hunger shall be satisfied[60] and, at the same time, enjoy the infinite satisfaction of table fellowship with the righteous, with the "fathers," and perhaps with the Son of man, if not with God himself. But one should not indulge prematurely in this prospect or take it for granted that one would be among those blessed ones who were to enjoy it. How one responded to the message of the Kingdom in the meantime was what now mattered (Luke 14:15–35). Men must seek the Kingdom of God and His righteousness, do His will, respond with mercy, forgiveness, helpfulness to their

---

55. In the Old Testament, the angelic beings or "sons of God," if somewhat tamed or demythologized (e.g., Gen. 6:1–4), were not thought of as phantasms but as having physical bodies. See, for instance, Gen. 19:1–3; Tobit 6:5; but cf. Tobit 12:19.

56. The hope for the "Messianic Banquet" appears as early as Isa. 25:6. Presumably, those to be gathered from the ends of heaven would be the righteous dead of earlier generations. Jesus says nothing about the risen dead of previous generations being assigned to Gehenna at the Judgment. In Luke 14:14 he refers only to "the resurrection of the righteous."

57. Matt. 8:11 = Luke 13:28 f.; Luke 22:30a; cf. Luke 14:15.

58. Mark 14:25 = Matt. 26:29 = Luke 22:17 f.; cf. Luke 22:16.

59. See sec. 14 of this study.

60. Luke 6:21; cf. 16:25.

neighbors. Those who do seek God's Kingdom above all else and live accordingly shall receive it, and there receive all such things as food and drink and clothing "as well" (Matt. 6:33 = Luke 12:31).

The fate of the unresponsive.—Not all would enter the Kingdom of God. Some would stand before the judgment throne of the Son of man and be found wanting: "Not everyone who says to me 'Lord, Lord,' shall enter the Kingdom of heaven; but he who does the will of my Father who is in heaven . . . " (Matt. 7:21).

Jesus understood the situation of his hearers to be highly precarious, a matter of life and death: "The gate is wide and the way is easy that leads to destruction" (Matt. 7:13). The exact fate of those who would be condemned at the Judgment is not certain: eternal torment or extinction? Perhaps the former. In either case, it would be terrible. Men would be "thrown into Gehenna, where their worm does not die, and the fire is not quenched, for everyone will be salted with fire."[61] There—in Gehenna, the "furnace of fire" or "the outer darkness"—"men will weep and gnash their teeth."[62] Luke reports that Jesus expected the misery of those in Gehenna to be compounded by seeing the righteous in enjoyment of the blessings of life in the Kingdom of God (Luke 13:28; cf. 16:23–27). At any rate, those who would not be found fit for the Kingdom, and of these there would be many (Matt. 7:13 = Luke 13:24), would forever be excluded from it:

> But he who hears [my words] and does not do them is like a
>   man who built a house on the ground without a foundation;
> against which the stream broke, and immediately it fell, and
>   the ruin of that house was great (Luke 6:49 = Matt. 7:26 f.).

61. Mark 9:47–49 = Matt. 5:29 f. = Matt. 18:9; cf. Isa. 66:24; *Enoch* 103:7 f.

62. Matt. 8:12 = Luke 13:28; Matt. 13:42, 50; 22:13; 24:51; 25:30, 41, 46. Matthew may have emphasized this severe prospect for parenetic purposes, but such is also indicated in Mark and Luke. There is no reason, other than the interpreter's wishes, for supposing that Jesus did not hold this fate before his hearers. Their response to his message would determine their final destiny: it was a matter of life and death. See Alan M. Fairhurst, "The Problem Posed by the Severe Sayings Attributed to Jesus in the Synoptic Gospels," *SJT* 23 (1970):77–91.

7. JESUS' BELIEFS ABOUT GOD AND MAN

Everything Jesus said and did evidences his beliefs about God. But he rarely talked about God without also referring implicitly or explicitly to man, nor did he talk about the human situation without also referring to God. The Kingdom of God was coming. Men should repent. Men should be merciful, for God is merciful. What should a man do? That which is the will of God.

Some fairly definite inferences can be drawn as to Jesus' beliefs about God. The Rich "Young" Man asked Jesus, "Good teacher, what must I do to inherit eternal life?" Jesus responded, "Why do you call me good? No one is good but God alone" (Mark 10:17 f.=Luke 18:18 f.). The goodness of God is radically different from that of man, including Jesus himself.

Jesus understood God to be both radically merciful and radically righteous. His mercy, love, or forgiveness is universal, all-inclusive: it does not distinguish, in this age, between the righteous and the unrighteous. On both, God bestows the blessings of sun and rain (Matt. 5:45); He is kind to the ungrateful and selfish (Luke 6:35). Therefore, Jesus exhorts his hearers, they also must be all-inclusive in their love; they must love not only their friends, but also their enemies if they would be the sons of the Most High (Matt. 5:44–45, 48=Luke 6:27, 35 f.). Since they pray for God's forgiveness, they must also forgive those who have offended them.[63] One must be ready to forgive even the repeated offender, the one who sins against you seven times a day, or seventy times seven times (Matt. 18:21–23=Luke 17:4).

What God most desires and requires of man is mercy, love, concern for the well-being of one another. This is more important than "sacrifice" or the keeping of the prescribed practices of law and tradition (Matt. 9:13=12:7; Mark 2:23–28 and parallels). God's love and mercy were not confined to humanity. Though men value them as having only a slight monetary value, not one sparrow is forgotten by God. But if God values sparrows, how much more does he value persons? (Matt. 10:29–31=Luke 12:6 f.). God cares for the needs of the birds of the air, and for the grass and flowers of the field, but to Him, people are of more value than these, and He will care that much more for them (Matt.

63. Mark 11:25 = Matt. 6:12 = Luke 11:4a; Matt. 6:14 f.; 18:23–35.

6:25–30 = Luke 12:22–28). This is not to say that man is inherently good—this is a myth of modern liberal culture. In Jesus' view, man is evil (Matt. 7:11 = Luke 11:13; cf. Gen. 6:5; 8:12). But though men are evil, they know how to give good gifts to their children. How much more will God, who alone is good, give good gifts to those who ask Him? Therefore, those who ask will receive the blessings of life in the Kingdom of God; those who seek it will find it.[64] God will hear the prayers of those who call on him to bring his Kingdom.[65]

But God is also radically righteous. Not all will be forgiven at the time of the Great Judgment. People will be judged by the same standard they have applied in judging others (Matt. 7:1 f. = Luke 6:37 f.). Jesus was aware of the tendency of humans to be blind to failings in themselves which they so readily detect in others: "Why do you see the speck of sawdust in your brother's eye, but do not notice the log that is in your own eye?" (Matt. 7:3–5 = Luke 6:41 f.). Blessed are the meek, the merciful, the peacemakers: they will inherit the earth, obtain mercy, and be called the sons of God (Matt. 5:5–9). By implication, those who are not so characterized will not receive these blessings. Men can be good enough to bring forth good, and evil enough to produce evil (Matt. 12:33–35 = Luke 6:43–45). There is a world of difference.

Not all will enter the Kingdom of God. One must truly seek it, and those who seek must repent and do the merciful and righteous will of God.[66] God is righteous, not a doddering "man upstairs" who "will forgive because it is his business to forgive." Those found unfit for entering the Kingdom of God would be excluded from it. And fitness for the Kingdom meant that men must make the radical choice for God and His Kingdom, against all other masters, ties, and loyalties in this world. It would not be enough to keep the Law or even the oral tradition: "Unless your righteousness exceeds that of the scribes and the Pharisees, you will never enter the Kingdom of heaven" (Matt. 5:20). But there is no indication that Jesus had in mind that the deeds of each man during his lifetime would be weighed in a juridical balance. God's forgiveness and righteousness overlap or interpenetrate. God would forgive men for what they

64. Matt. 6:33 = Luke 12:31; Matt. 7:7–11 = Luke 11:9–13.
65. Matt. 6:10 = Luke 11:2; Luke 12:32; 18:1–8.
66. Matt. 7:21–23 = Luke 6:46; cf. Luke 13:26 f.; Matt. 7:24–27 = Luke 6:47–49; Matt. 25:31–46.

did in the past if they would now repent and turn to Him and the doing of His will in the time that remained before the Judgment. This seems to be the main point in the Matthean parable of the laborers in the vineyard (Matt. 20:1–16). There will be joy in heaven for the sinner who repents (Matt. 18:12–14; Luke 15:4–10). But repent men must, else they will perish (Luke 13:1–5). They must keep the faith, "watch," so that they will be found ready for the coming of the Judge and the Judgment, and this could happen at any time.[67]

God's love for man and His righteousness are finally represented in the two different situations which Jesus expected Him to bring about. In the Kingdom of God, the power of the Evil One would be forever bound or broken: there would be no more sickness, pain, hunger, misery, or death. Instead, men and women would live like the angels, they would see God, and forever share the blessings of life in the Age to come, material as well as spiritual: food, drink, companionship with the righteous of all generations. But the unforgiving, the unrighteous, the unrepentant would forever be excluded from these joys, perhaps with the added misery of knowing that they had missed their great opportunity through their indifference to those in need around them in their life in the Old world.[68]

That Jesus was addressing himself primarily to Jewish men and women may need to be mentioned. That he healed a Roman centurian's slave (Matt. 8:5–13 = Luke 7:1–10) is exceptional, as indicated by his initial unresponsiveness to the request of the "Canaanite" or Syrophoenician woman (Mark 7:24–30 = Matt. 15:21–28). Matthew is probably correct in reporting that Jesus sent the Twelve to proclaim the coming of the Kingdom of God and to cast out demons within the territory and populace of "Israel" (Matt. 10:6, 23) or Galilee. But that at least some Gentiles might find place in the Kingdom of God is suggested in the sayings about the men of Nineveh and the Queen of the South, Sodom and Gomorrah, and, perhaps, the saying about the many who would come from East and West (and North and South) to sit at the table in the Kingdom of God. For after all, the Kingdom of God

67. Mark 13:33–37 and parallels; Luke 21:34–36; Matt. 24:37–50 = Luke 17:26 f., 34 f.; Luke 12:39 f., 42–46; Matt. 25:1–13; Matt. 25:14–30 = Luke 19:12–27.

68. Matt. 25:1–13; Matt. 25:14–30 = Luke 19:12–26; Matt. 25:31–46; Luke 16:22–26.

would not only come in Israel: the whole earth would be "reborn" or transformed.

Men were evil, but God was good. But men were not so evil as to be unable to respond with repentance to the message that the Kingdom of God had come near. And God was not so "good" as to view with indifference the indifference of men to His will and to one another. He loved His whole creation. But only those who loved Him and one another would enter the New world that was about to be created.

8. JESUS' BELIEFS ABOUT HIMSELF

Jesus rebuked the Rich "Young" Man for calling him good: "No one is good but God alone" (Mark 10:17 f.=Luke 18:18 f.). The implication is not so much that Jesus considered himself sinful, but rather that he did not consider himself to be God. Either may have been the reason for Matthew's attempt to "correct" the saying: "Why do you ask me about what is good?"[69] The Jesus of the first three Gospels does not equate himself with God after the fashion of the Jesus of the Fourth Gospel (e.g., John 14:7 ff.; 17:11; 20:28).

Jesus prays to God, addresses Him as "Father," and has his followers address Him similarly (Matt. 6:9=Luke 11:2). He differentiates between his own desires and hopes and what God may will to cause to happen (Mark 14:32–36 and parallels), and does not claim to know exactly when the final events will take place: only the Father knows that (Mark 13:32=Matt. 24:36).

That Jesus did not proclaim himself to be "the Messiah" or "Christ" is well known, at least in scholarly circles. It is not apparent from the evidence—the Jewish and Christian literature of the period—that the Jewish people as a whole were even looking for "the Messiah." The one who was to come first, the herald of the Judgment and the Coming age, was Elijah. It may be that Jesus understood himself, in part at least, in terms of the Elijah role, in which case he also understood that he shared it with the

69. See Matt. 19:16 f.; also Matthew's "explanation" as to why Jesus was baptized by John (3:14 f.); and Matt. 11:11b = Luke 7:28b, which perhaps was added by the church lest Jesus' tribute to John (the greatest among those born of women) seem to overshadow his own importance. See, however, KGST, pp. 57–65.

Baptist.[70] He may have meant to discredit either the Messiah expectation of some of his contemporaries or the idea (attributed to the scribes) that the Messiah must be a descendent of David: "David himself calls him Lord; so how is he his son?"[71] If Jesus accepts the validity of the passage (Ps. 110:1) as a prophecy referring to the future Messiah, as may have been the case, his point would be that the Christ (= Messiah), whoever he was, would not be a descendent of David. Despite the elaborate (though somewhat divergent) genealogies with which Jesus is provided by the authors of Matthew and Luke (Matt. 1:1–17; Luke 3:23–38), it may have been that Jesus was not himself a descendent of David. It would seem that either Jesus was a "son" (descendent) of David, as claimed by Matthew and Luke, in which case (according to Mark 12:35 ff. and parallels) he may have meant that he himself was not the Messiah; or, if Matthew and Luke were in error and he was not a descendent of David, his meaning at Mark 12:35 ff. may have been that he himself was not on this account disqualified from holding that office. We cannot be certain whether Jesus understood himself to be the Messiah or not. But, as will be seen, his manner of entering Jerusalem, seated on an ass's colt, suggests at least the possibility that he came to that city as one acting in accordance with the messianic prophecy of Zech. 9:9.[72] Whether he acknowledged to the High Priest that he was the Messiah we cannot be certain. According to Mark 14:62, he did. But the parallels are not so definite even about this (Matt. 26:64= Luke 22:70).

He did probably regard himself as the one who would come or be revealed as the Son of man, the Judge, who would preside at the

70. See secs. 9 and 20 of this study.

71. Mark 12:35–37 and parallels. The assumptions basic to Jesus' argument are that David was the author of Ps. 110 and that "my lord" in 110:1 referred to the future Messiah. As in the case of his argument, from the Old Testament disclosure of God to Moses as the God of Abraham, Isaac, and Jacob (Ex. 3:15) to the conclusion that He is the God of the living (Mark 12:18–27 and parallels), Jesus' reasoning is along rabbinical-rationalizing lines rather than historical-critical ones. He would not, of course, have had any reason to suspect that David might not have written the psalm, or that its *Sitz im Leben* (if not origin) was in the ancient Israelite festival in which Kings were enthroned. But cf. Schweitzer, *Kingdom of God*, pp. 104–5: "The solution to the riddle is that the Messiah in his earthly existence is subordinate to David as his successor, but in the coming Kingdom, as the Messiah, he is above him."

72. See secs. 17, 18, 22, and 23 of this study.

Great Judgment. Certain interpreters have recently urged, though with differing arguments, that the Son of man sayings were all composed and inserted into the tradition by the early Church. Certainly this is possible. In New Testament research, all things are possible, but not all things are likely. The request of James and John for special seats beside Jesus "in your glory" (Mark 10:35–40 = Matt. 20:20–23) does not mention the Son of man, but there seems little question as to the authenticity of this unit of tradition. Here neither the aspiring brothers nor Jesus himself seem to doubt that he will be enthroned "in glory," either at the Judgment or in the Kingdom of God. "Glory" is associated with the appearance of the Son of man in other synoptic sayings attributed to Jesus.[73]

That Jesus twice appears to acknowledge the title "Messiah" but then immediately speaks of the Son of man (Mark 8:29 ff.; 14:61 f. and parallels) has led some interpreters to believe that Jesus preferred the latter title for himself. The fact that he never explicitly identifies himself as or with the Son of man who is to come as Judge at the end of the Present age has led others, most notably Bultmann, to propose that Jesus probably was thinking of someone other than himself as the one who would come as Son of man. The problem of the two, three, or four possible meanings that "son of man" may have had in the several synoptic sayings attributed to Jesus has been and still is one of the most discussed topics in the field of New Testament research.[74] In a great many of the sayings (especially those first reported by Mark), Jesus speaks of himself as "son of man"; he does not refer in these sayings to future power and glory but instead to the suffering and trials which he, as son of man, must endure. On the other hand, in numerous other sayings, he refers to the future glory and power that will characterize the coming of the Son of man, but without claiming that he himself is the same as this future Son of man. One could plausibly infer that he used the term "son of man" to signify—perhaps as a mystery which only he himself needed to understand—that the two were one, that he who now in his present

---

73. Mark 13:26 = Matt. 24:30 = Luke 21:27; Matt. 25:31; cf. Luke 17:22 ff. This idea was derived, probably, from the language of Dan. 7:13 f.

74. See Weiss, *Jesus' Proclamation*, p. 117n85. Norman Perrin's conclusion that all references to the future coming of the Son of man must have originated in the early Church seems premature and influenced by ideological considerations.

ministry was "servant," with no place to lay his head, would at the dawning of the Age to come be manifested in glory as the great Judge. The contrast between his present lowliness and future exaltation would correspond to the contrast between the present conditions of the poor, the lowly, the *am-ha aretz*, and their prospective life of splendor: the last shall be first and the first last. Similarly, the mustard seed "is the smallest of all the seeds on earth," but "becomes the greatest of all shrubs" (Mark 4:30–32 and parallels). Something of the sort is certainly implied in the description of the Great Judgment in Matt. 25:31–46: here the Judge (or "King") identifies himself with those who, in the Present age, were hungry, thirsty, a stranger, naked, sick, in prison: "I was hungry and you gave me food. . . . As you did it to one of the least of these my brethren, you did it to me." The saying about acknowledging Jesus before men may represent a similar understanding. The Lukan version, which refers to the Son of man, may be the earlier: "And I tell you, every one who acknowledges me before men, the Son of man also will acknowledge before the angels of God . . . " (Luke 12:8 f.; cf. Matt. 10:32 f.). This does not say how Jesus is to be acknowledged: as Teacher, Son of man, or Messiah, or by hearing and doing his words. The sense seems to be that one who responds to Jesus as bearer of God's message with believing and doing will be sustained by the Son of man at the Great Judgment.[75] This is certainly the understanding in Luke 13:26 f. (cf. Matt. 7:22 f.): "Then you will say, 'We ate and drank in your presence, and you taught in our streets.'" The clear implication is that the coming Son of man first will have lived, during the days of the Old world, with those who would then come before him as Judge at the end of the Present age.

The saying at the Last Supper also implies the contrast between the undistinguished situation of Jesus and his followers now, and the glory and joy of their reunion in the Coming age, though this does not refer to the Judgment or Son of man. Here, as at the meal in the wilderness, Jesus was celebrating in advance the table fellowship that would be fulfilled in the Kingdom of God.[76] The whole of Jesus' activity, in fact, was a kind of anticipatory celebration of the joys of the Coming age: "The son of man came

75. Cf. Matt. 7:21–27 and Lukan parallels; Luke 13:1–9; Mark 8:36—9:1 and parallels.
76. See secs. 14 and 24 of this study.

eating and drinking" (Matt. 11:19=Luke 7:34). But in his present life, his experience was one of hardship, homelessness, and dishonor.

The bridegroom saying also implies that Jesus was, at least with his own disciples, enjoying a preliminary celebration of that which was to be fulfilled in the Coming age: "Can the wedding guests fast while the bridegroom is with them?" (Mark 2:19 and parallels). The terms "bridegroom" (*numphios*) and "wedding guests" or "bridegroom's attendants" (*hoi huioi tou numphōnos*) indicate that the wedding has not yet taken place, and the bridegroom has yet to be installed as husband. The implication is that Jesus, the son of man in lowliness, has yet to be installed in the office of the Son of man in glory, but he and his followers are already anticipating that joyful time, soon to be fulfilled. Wedding, of course, is another symbol or image for the Kingdom of God and its joys (Matt. 22:1-14; 25:1-13).

Similarly, on the way to Jerusalem, Jesus' disciples, who suppose that the Kingdom of God is about to appear (Luke 19:11), argue as to which of them will be the greatest (Mark 9:34 and parallels) and vie for the seats of greater glory (Mark 10:35 ff.; cf. Matt. 20:20 ff.). On both of these occasions, as Mark tells the story, the disciples are prompted to think of the glories of the coming era by Jesus' references to his own impending death and resurrection—a strange and crass reaction, unless they really believed that despite or because of Jesus' impending death and resurrection they would soon be together in the Kingdom of God! In the case of the bridegroom saying, Jesus proclaims that "the days will come when the bridegroom is taken away"—still before the "wedding" (Mark 2: 20). Jesus' saying over the "cup" at the Last Supper also suggests that he understood that he first must die. It is assumed by many, perhaps a majority, of critics that the "passion predictions" were not spoken by Jesus, but inserted by the Church in an attempt to explain the troublesome fact of his death. This may be correct. On the other hand, there seems no doubt that Jesus expected that he and his followers would have to experience the "tribulation" before they could share the joys of life in the Kingdom of God, unless, of course, God might be prevailed upon to eliminate the tribulation from the program of divinely revealed events to come.[77] In the same setting in which everyone, including Jesus, anticipated his forth-

77. Matt. 6:13 = Luke 11:4; Mark 14:35 f., 38.

coming enthronement in glory, Jesus identified the son of man (apparently himself) as the servant who came to serve and give his life as a ransom for many (Mark 10:45). The "servant" of Isa. 52–53 who was "cut off out of the land of the living" yet "bore the sin of many" also was to be vindicated:

He shall see his offspring,
   he shall prolong his days,
the will of the LORD shall prosper in his hand;
   he shall see the fruit of the travail of his soul and be satisfied. . . .
I will divide him a portion with the great,
   and he shall divide the spoil with the strong (Isa. 53:10–12).

Not only the early church but Jesus himself may have seen here[78] a disclosure of the divine plan. At any rate, the "passion predictions" refer to the necessity of the suffering and death of the Son of man, and in Mark 9:12, Jesus states that it is so written in the Scriptures.

If Jesus understood that he must first die before he could come as the Son of man in power and glory, his thinking was completely logical and coherent. Now he was the son of man, servant. Then he would be the glorious Son of man, Judge. How could he proceed from the one condition to the other? He, like all else, would need to be transformed; in order to become "like the angels" he too would need to experience a "rebirth." Even the greatest of those born of women, John the Baptist, who had come as Elijah, with whom Jesus' own career was so closely related, would have to be transformed before entering the Kingdom of God. Perhaps he had earlier thought, as he still hoped and prayed, that the world transformation might occur without the necessity of the tribulation and his own death. But by death and resurrection he would, indeed, be transformed, as would all others "in the resurrection." If he was to become the glorious Son of man, coming on the clouds of heaven to judge the earth, he could become such by the hard way of death and resurrection. How else, in fact, could he hope to mount the clouds of heaven that he might descend upon them? He who called on others to give up all they had in this world—including life—

78. Jesus' thinking and acting may have been determined also by certain passages in the book of Zechariah. See secs. 18, 20, 22, 24, and 25 of this study.

for the sake of the Kingdom of God was himself prepared to give up all that he might become the Son of man who was to come.

The Son of man was to come at the dawning of the Kingdom of God. Before men could enter the Kingdom, they must first pass by the judgment seat of the Son of man. The secret or mystery of the Kingdom of God then became fused with the mystery of Jesus' own identity and passion. By his death he would undergo—perhaps with others, at all events by himself—the "cup" of "tribulation," and by his resurrection would be transformed into the Son of man, seated at the right hand of God. There he would be ready to come to judge the earth at the time known only by God. After his death and resurrection, it was only natural that his followers, who still awaited the coming of the Kingdom of God and the Son of man, should now also await the coming of Jesus as Son of man and pray not only "Thy Kingdom come!" but also "Our Lord, come!," "Come, Lord Jesus!" (I Cor. 16:22; Rev. 22:20).[79]

79. The Church, quite early, came to look for Jesus' return as the Christ or Messiah, perhaps understanding that he had become such through or after his resurrection (Rom. 1:3 f.; Phil. 3:20; Acts 2:36).

III

Jesus' Galilean Ministry

J ESUS' beliefs and expectations are not only evidenced in
his preaching and sayings, but also in his actions and inter-
actions with others. On some occasions, sayings are reported that
provide a clue to his intentions or his understanding of a situation.
At other times, one can only try to infer the meaning or purpose
of his actions. In many instances, recognition of his eschatological
beliefs renders his otherwise enigmatic or incoherent activities, in
both Galilee and Jerusalem, completely intelligible.

Following the synoptic framework, which is largely grounded
upon Mark, historians of Jesus' public activity traditionally distinguish between his Galilean ministry and his ministry in Jerusalem. Often it is asserted, despite the reports that Jesus was followed enthusiastically by large crowds, that his Galilean ministry
was a failure. Also, interpreters are generally at a loss to give a
coherent explanation of Jesus' decision to go to Jerusalem. Both
periods are usually related only vaguely, at best, to his eschatological beliefs and declarations.

One should not make too much of the distinction between these
periods. It is quite possible that some of the episodes and sayings
placed in one setting really belong in the other, if not somewhere
else entirely. But for the most part there seems to be little reason
to suppose that the traditions have been displaced. If they have
been, it makes little difference, for from beginning to end, Jesus'
sayings, actions, and intentions consistently reveal and are integral
to his belief that certain eschatological events were already taking
place while the decisive ones were yet to occur. The Kingdom of
God could come at any time. For this reason, no particular significance is attached to the order in which these traditions are presented, either in Chapter III or Chapter IV of this study. What
especially interests us in both of these chapters is the correlation of

47

Jesus' words and the events in which he participated. In both, as they converge, we can see a fairly clear pattern of understanding in regard to the purposes of God, his own role, and the situation of his disciples and contemporaries.

9. THE COMING OF THE ONE WHO IS TO COME: ELIJAH

The expectation that Elijah would return as the final prophet and preacher of repentance before the "Day of the Lord"—the coming of the Messiah and/or the Messianic Age—is a well-attested feature of first-century Jewish apocalyptic hope. Its biblical roots go back at least as far as the second century BC (Mal. 3:1 f., 4:5 f.; Sirach 48:9 f.). Subsequent Jewish interpretations of these passages make clear the understanding that Elijah's preaching would prepare Israel, through repentance, for the coming of the final Judgment and the Messiah (or God), and/or the Messianic Age.[1] In later literature, Elijah himself is depicted as a messianic figure: "It is he alone who brings down the rulers of the world, who redeems Israel, and finally brings to pass the resurrection of the dead."[2]

There is no evidence that any first-century Jews expected Elijah to come as the forerunner or herald of the Messiah. The passages in Malachi and Sirach speak of his coming "before the great and terrible day of the Lord," "at the appointed time," "before [the wrath of God] breaks out in fury." Of course, those who looked for the coming of a Messiah in connection with the beginning of the Messianic Age would have expected the Messiah to appear after the coming of Elijah. But specific reference to Elijah as forerunner of the Messiah is not attested prior to the second-century *Dialogue with Trypho* by Justin (8:4; 49:1).[3]

That the scribes of Jesus' day looked for the coming of Elijah

1. Billerbeck, 4:779 ff., 1:597.
2. Ibid., 4:783, 792 ff.; see also J. Jeremias in *TWNT*, 2:935 f., 942 f.
3. Even this evidence is questionable. Justin, of course, knows that John baptized Jesus, and argues that since John was Elijah, Trypho should recognize that Jesus was the Christ (*Dial.* 49:2—51:3). The belief he attributes to Trypho—that Elijah was to anoint the Messiah—seems to set the stage for this argument. But did Trypho (= second-century Jews) really believe that Elijah would anoint the Messiah?

"first"—"to restore all things"—we learn from the New Testament (Mark 9:11 = Matt. 17:10). Here it is taken as a matter of scriptural or dogmatic necessity: "first Elijah must [dei] come."

Jesus' concurrence with this doctrine is indicated in Mark 9:12, and in the following verse, he goes on to make the startling announcement that Elijah has already come! Mark evidently understood that Jesus referred to John the Baptist, for in 1:2–4 Mark introduces the Baptist as the Messenger or "Coming One" of Mal. 3:1. Matthew reports that Jesus publicly and explicitly identified the Baptist as Elijah (11:13–15), and adds that the disciples subsequently came to understand that he recognized John as Elijah (17:13). "Q" tradition also indicates that this was Jesus' understanding (Matt. 11:10 = Luke 7:27). Luke adds that John's role as Elijah was revealed to his father even before the child was conceived (Luke 1:16 f.). However, here we are in the realm of later embellishment or legend.

Jesus' identification of John as Elijah raises many intriguing questions.[4] The point of interest here is that, in recognizing John as Elijah, Jesus gives unmistakable evidence of his understanding that the last days of the Present age have arrived. The meaning of the seemingly enigmatic "Q" saying about the Law and the prophets (Matt. 11:13 = Luke 16:16a) is precisely this: with the arrival of John, the days anticipated in Scripture had come, namely, the days of the Coming One, Elijah. Until John, there was only prophecy. With the coming of John began fulfillment: Elijah had come. This may well be the point of the reference to "the time" in Mark's summary of Jesus' Galilean preaching following the appearance—and arrest—of John: "The time is fulfilled, and the Kingdom of God is near; repent" (Mark 1:15).

The appearance of John–Elijah did not, of course, mean that the Kingdom of God had come. Elijah was to come "first," "before" the Day of the Lord. But the fact that Elijah had come must have meant to Jesus that the coming of the Judgment and Kingdom would not be far away. And this is precisely what Jesus proclaimed.

The arrest and execution of the Baptist–Elijah may have posed a special problem for Jesus. It is not known whether the ideas of a final battle between Elijah (and Enoch) and the Anti-Christ, and

4. See, for example, J. A. T. Robinson, "Elijah, John, and Jesus," in his *Twelve New Testament Studies*, SBT no. 34 (London: SCM, 1962), pp. 28–52; Schweitzer, *Kingdom of God*, pp. 75–80.

the martyrdom of the returned Elijah (and Enoch), were current in Jesus' time.[5] That Jesus' ministry began, according to Mark, after John's arrest suggests that Jesus may have seen his role as a continuation of Elijah–John's work. John's death evidently had eschatological meaning for Jesus: the fate of Elijah–John is directly related to that of the Son of man (Mark 9:12). Likewise, in the enigmatic "Q" saying about the Baptist and the Kingdom of God (Matt. 11:12 = Luke 16:16b), the death of the Baptist is presupposed. Since, or perhaps beginning with, the martyrdom of Elijah–John, the Kingdom had been on its way. The conflict between the power of God and the forces of the Evil One had begun.[6] Jesus evidently associated his own ministry with that of the Baptist (Matt. 11:16–19; Mark 11:27–33). Schweitzer and several others thought that Jesus regarded Elijah–John as the forerunner of the Messiah. It is possible, however, that Jesus regarded himself as Elijah–John's successor or colleague, as the biblical Elisha took up the mantle of Elijah after his removal from the earth, or as Enoch was expected to be Elijah's co-worker at the end of the age.[7] A relatively late tradition suggests the identification of Enoch with the Son of man (*Enoch* 70–71). Jesus used the term Son of man regularly in speaking of himself. It is just possible that Mark 9:12 f. implies Jesus' familiarity with the tradition about the martyrdom of Elijah and Enoch and, further, his assumption, for a while at least, of the role of Enoch.

It can be assumed that the Baptist did not know that he was Elijah, even if the explicit disavowal attributed to him in John 1:21 is secondary.[8] There is no reason to suppose that it had occurred to the Baptist or anyone else that he might be Elijah. Baptizing was not part of the program of either the historical or the apocalyptic Elijah. John proclaims that one is coming who, like

5. J. Jeremias thinks they were (*TWNT*, 2:942 f.). See also Rev. 11:3–13.
6. See Betz, *What Do We Know?*, pp. 53–54, and *KGST*, pp. 36–42.
7. See sec. 2n15 of this study. The return of Elijah and Enoch was also to take place before the time of Judgment (*Enoch* 89:52; 90:31; cf. IV Ezra 6:26). Note also the relation between Moses and Joshua in leading Israel into the Land of Promise, or of David and Solomon in establishing the throne and Temple (II Sam. 7:12 ff.): the latter would complete the task begun by the former.
8. Werner regards it as a feature of the Fourth Gospel's de-eschatologizing program: If John was not Elijah, the problem of the delay of the parousia disappears (Martin Werner, *The Formation of Christian Dogma* [London: Adam and Charles Black, 1957], p. 70).

"the coming one" of Mal. 3:1 ff., would purify with fire. Nothing indicates that he expected the coming of "the Messiah," but he may well have been looking for the coming of Elijah! After his arrest, John evidently heard of Jesus' activity and sent messengers to inquire of Jesus whether he, Jesus, was "the coming one" (*ho erchomenos*) (Matt. 11:3). John may have understood that "the coming one" was Elijah. It is Jesus who explicitly identifies John with these titles or roles, both in Matt. 11:14 and in the "Q" explanation (Matt. 11:10=Luke 7:27): John, not Jesus, is the "messenger," Elijah "the one who must come." Elijah, of course, is not only prophet, but more than prophet: he is the greatest of those born of women, the most important person to appear in the Present age (Matt. 11:9, 11 and parallels).[9] It is often asserted that Matt. 11:11b is secondary. This may be, for Christians might have found it inconceivable that Jesus had accorded someone other than himself such a distinction. But if the latter part of the verse is authentic, it would mean only that those in the coming Kingdom of God will surpass even the greatest man of the Present age. For Jesus, the arrival of Elijah was an eschatological event of the greatest consequence, for it signified the imminence of the Judgment (Day of the Lord) and the Messianic Age.

10. THE PREACHING OF REPENTANCE

The Old Testament prophets generally understood and proclaimed that by repentance—"turning" or "returning" to God and his Law—Israel, or at any rate those Israelites who "turned," might yet be spared the destruction otherwise in store for them on the impending Day of Yahweh. This understanding is expressed thematically in Jeremiah: "Return, faithless Israel": "O Jerusalem, wash your heart from wickedness, that you may be saved."[10] By returning or repentance, Israel was to prepare herself for participation in the blessings which God would bring in the time of redemption.[11]

In rabbinical literature also, it is understood that the time for Israel to repent was before the coming of the Messiah and/or the

9. For exegesis, see *KGST*, pp. 57–65.
10. Jer. 3:12; 4:14; see also 3:3–18, 22; 4:1–4; 6:16; 7:5 ff.; 18:7 f.; Amos 5:6, 14 f.; Ezek. 18:30–32.
11. E.g., Hos. 10:12; 14:1–7; Isa. 30:15.

Coming age. In both prophetic and rabbinic conceptions, it would be too late afterwards.

Various rabbinical sayings propose that, by repentance (and/or keeping the commandments or doing good deeds), the coming of the Messiah or Messianic Age can be hastened: "Rabbi Jose the Galilean (c. 110) said, 'Good is repentance, for it brings to pass the [messianic] redemption.' "[12] This idea is also implied in Acts 3:19: "Repent therefore, and turn again . . . that times of refreshing may come from the presence of the Lord," and also, perhaps, in Rom. 16:19–20a. On the basis of this idea, Schweitzer maintained that Jesus believed that the movement of repentance, awakened by the preaching of the Baptist and carried forward in his own preaching and that of his disciples, would exert pressure on the coming of the Kingdom. Such, Schweitzer suggested, is the meaning of the saying in Matt. 11:12 about the "men of violence." The coming of the Kingdom would be hastened or constrained by the force of repentance.[13] This saying is capable of more plausible interpretation, however, and in the absence of any other evidence to that effect, it seems unlikely that Jesus held to this particular theory about repentance.

There can be no doubt, however, that Jesus regarded "repentance as preparation for the coming of the Kingdom" in that it prepared those who repented for entrance into that era of blessedness.[14] Surely no impenitent, unconverted sinners would enter the Kingdom!

According to Mark and to "Q" and "M" traditions,[15] the preaching of repentance began with John the Baptist. John's baptizing, from which his popular title "the Baptizer" or "Baptist" was derived, is described as a "baptism of repentance for the remission of sins" (Mark 1:4=Luke 3:3). In Matt. 3:7 f.=Luke 3:7 f., it is clear that John understood this baptism as an eschatological sacrament, marking those who genuinely repented in the face of the impending "wrath to come." Matt. 3:2 specifies that it was the nearness of the Kingdom of God which John proclaimed as the occasion for his

12. Billerbeck, 1:599; see also 162 ff. and 599 ff. See also *Testament of Dan* 6:3 f.
13. Schweitzer, *Mystery*, p. 147; *Kingdom of God*, pp. 123–24.
14. Schweitzer, *Mystery*, p. 53; cf. *Kingdom of God*, pp. 124, 81–88. See also Paul S. Minear, *Commands of Christ* (Nashville: Abingdon, 1972), esp. pp. 21–29.
15. Mark 1:4; Matt. 3:8 = Luke 3:8; Matt. 3:2, 11.

call to repentance. In any case, John's preaching about the One coming after him, whether Elijah or Messiah, establishes his belief that the Coming age was soon to begin.

Repentance is also the central theme in the message of Jesus and his disciples. This is the case not only where the call to repentance is explicitly joined with the announcement that the Kingdom of God has come near,[16] but also in several other instances of Jesus' and the disciples' preaching.[17]

It may well be that Matt. 10:16–23a reflects the persecution experienced by the early Church. It comes nearly verbatim from the Markan apocalypse (13:9–13). But the admonition in 10:23a to "flee to the next town" and the warning that the missionary disciples "will not have gone through all the towns of Israel before the Son of man comes" fit well into the context of Matt. 9:37—10:15, where the Twelve are explicitly charged to proclaim the nearness of the Kingdom. Their mission is urgent (cf. Matt. 9:37 f.; 10:7 ff. and parallels); there is no time to lose (10:23), and they are to hurry on with their work in order to do what they can before it is too late. It is not clear whether the gesture of shaking the dust from their feet upon leaving was to imply doom or haste. In either case, those who hear the warning but refuse to heed have had their chance. The disciple–missionaries must press on in order to extend this last chance for repentance to the other towns of Israel, or as many of them as possible, before the "harvest"—the Judgment and the Kingdom of God—comes.

The basis for repentance is recognition of the degree to which one has fallen short of the measure of righteousness and love which God demands and desires. The nearness of the Kingdom makes urgent the need for repentance. Soon it would be too late for repentance. The Semitic idiom "to turn" probably lies behind several of the sayings where the word "repent" may not appear in the Greek or English renderings. Those who heed the admonition to

---

16. Mark 1:15 = Matt. 4:17.

17. Mark 6:12; Luke 5:32; 13:1–5; 15:7, 10; Mark 10:15 = Matt. 18:3; cf. John 3:3, 5. Repentance is the fitting response to Jesus and his preaching implicit in Mark 4:12 = Matt. 13:15 and Matt. 12:41 = Luke 11:32. It is also apparently the response men should make to Jesus' and his disciples' preaching of "the gospel" or "good news" of the Kingdom of God (Matt. 4:23; 9:35; 10:7 = Luke 4:43; 8:1; 10:9, 11). Weiss concluded that Jesus' message was, in effect, "Repent, for the Kingdom of God has come near" (Jesus' Proclamation, pp. 65–66).

seek the Kingdom of God must turn to God and his righteousness and forsake all other masters, duties, even otherwise proper
responsibilities.[18] Schweitzer correctly characterized the whole of
Jesus' ethical "teaching" as an "ethic for the interim," an ethic of
repentance in preparation for entrance into the Kingdom of God
which was coming.[19]

The eschatological time for repentance has arrived. One does
not, by repenting, enter the Kingdom of God. But repentance is
the fitting response for men to make in the days that remain before the Kingdom of God comes, for then they will be judged
against the standard of God's righteousness (Matt. 6:33; cf. 5:20).
Only those who repent can pray for forgiveness of their sins, and
forgive the offenses of others, and only those who repent—who forgive and hope for forgiveness of their own sins by God—have any
reason to pray for the coming of his Kingdom (Matt. 6:10, 12=
Luke 11:2, 4).

11.   THE SPIRIT OF GOD AND PROPHECY

As evident both in the Old Testament and other Jewish sources,
by the time of Jesus, Jewish tradition had developed the idea that
the Spirit of God and, with it, the gift of prophecy had been taken
away. Prophecy was thought to have ceased with Malachi.[20] From
the standpoint of historical criticism, the last of the canonical
prophetic material comes from no later than the early part of the

18. E.g., Matt. 6:24 = Luke 16:13; Matt. 6:33 = Luke 12:31; Matt.
7:13 f. = Luke 13:23 f.; Matt. 8:21 f. = Luke 9:59; Matt. 10:34–39 and
parallels. See sec. 2 of this study.

19. What Schweitzer meant by "interim ethics" has generally been misrepresented. Such misrepresentations do not detract from the aptness of this
characterization, but only show the degree to which the eschatological interpretation of Jesus and his message has been opposed because of doctrinal
considerations. In this connection, see my articles "Interim Ethics," pp. 220–
33, and "Eschatology and Methodology," esp. pp. 175–84.

20. Eduard Schweizer et al., Spirit of God (London: A. & C. Black, 1960),
p. 13; Schweizer, "Gegenwart des Geistes und Eschatologische Hoffnung,"
in W. D. Davies and W. Daube, The Background of the New Testament
and Its Eschatology (Cambridge: At the University Press, 1964), p. 484;
George Foot Moore, Judaism (Cambridge: At the University Press, 1927),
1:240, 421; Walter Grundmann, Der Begriff der Kraft in der neutestament-
lichen Gedankenwelt (Stuttgart: W. Kohlhammer, 1932), p. 58.

second century,[21] and in theory (both Jewish and Christian), there had been no prophets since the fifth or sixth century BC.

It is implied at many points in the Old Testament that the gift of prophecy was a gift of the Spirit of God.[22] If the gift of prophecy has been restored, it is a sign that the Spirit of God has once more visited Israel. The outpouring or renewal of the gift of the Spirit was expected "afterward" or "in the latter days" which were to come "before the great and terrible day of the Lord comes" (Joel 2:28 f.; Isa. 59:21). The presence of the Spirit in prophecy or vision means, then, to one who knows these traditions that the last days of the Present age have come. That Jesus acknowledged the Baptist as prophet, let alone "more than prophet" (Matt. 11:9 = Luke 7:26), can only mean that he considered the last days of the Old age to have come.[23]

It is in Luke, especially, that the Spirit of God is presented in connection with prophecy. The angel announces to Zechariah that his son, John, "will be filled with the Holy Spirit even from his mother's womb," and minister to Israel in the role ("spirit and power") of Elijah (Luke 1:15 ff.). Here, the presence of the Spirit is specifically associated with John's appearance as Elijah. Possibly Luke had in mind both Joel 2:28 ff. and Mal. 4:5: the outpouring of the Spirit and the arrival of Elijah were both expected to take place "before the great and terrible day of the Lord comes." Luke does not confine the Spirit to the prophetic work of John (Elijah). Elizabeth, John's mother, and Zechariah, his father, are also "filled with the Holy Spirit" (Luke 1:41, 67) and prophesy, as does Simeon (Luke 2:26–35).

The Spirit comes most significantly, of course, upon Jesus "in bodily form," visible, presumably, to all (Luke 3:22), after which Jesus was "full of the Holy Spirit" (Luke 4:1; cf. parallels). After his temptation, he returned "in the power of the Spirit" (4:14) to

21. Although Daniel and Zech. 9–14, together with some of the interpolated prophetic oracles, were probably written in the second century BC, this material was attributed to earlier figures, both in order to lend the authority of antiquity (especially in the apocalyptic material) and, probably, because of the understanding that the era of prophecy was now over.

22. E.g., Num. 11:29; I Sam. 10:9–13; II Sam. 23:2; Isa. 61:1 ff. See Schweizer, *Spirit*, p. 7.

23. See Carl H. Kraeling, *John the Baptist* (New York: Scribner, 1951), pp. 141–45; J. E. Yates, *The Spirit and the Kingdom* (London: SPCK, 1963), p. 86; cf. Franklin W. Young, "Jesus the Prophet: A Re-examination," *JBL* 68 (1949):285–99.

Galilee, where in his "inaugural sermon" he turned, appropriately, to Isa. 61:1 ff. and announced to those about him that " 'Today this Scripture has been fulfilled in your hearing.' " By the latter phrase, it appears that Luke meant that it was the preaching or proclamation of Jesus which fulfilled the words of Scripture. His prophetic utterance fulfilled the prophecy about the penultimate times. Later on, Jesus reported a vision of Satan's destruction, probably prophetic in character (i.e., describing what is to happen in the future), and "rejoiced in the Holy Spirit" (Luke 10:17-21).[24] Luke probably understood the Holy Spirit to be the source of Jesus' vision.

In these Lukan traditions, it is to be noted that the Holy Spirit was thought to be present with or within individuals and, as in typical Old Testament and Jewish thought, in connection with prophetic powers of vision and speech.[25] Luke understood that the "latter days" when the gift of prophecy would be restored, when the Spirit would once more be poured out, had come. For Luke, the Spirit of God was present already in the prophetic utterances of certain of Jesus' immediate predecessors, in Jesus himself, and in the early Church. This does not mean, however, that Luke understood that the Kingdom of God or the Coming age had arrived.[26] Similarly, Paul and his Corinthian congregation interpreted the utterance of prophecy and tongues as the work of the Spirit (I Cor. 12–14). But it is quite clear that Paul considered these spiritual gifts to be operative and relevant only in that time remaining before "the perfect" (13:10), i.e., the Messianic Age, came.[27] Afterward, they would "pass away."

Mark 1:10 reports a vision experienced by Jesus in which he sees the Spirit descending upon himself. It is not certain that the Spirit is associated here with the gift of prophecy. In the Markan verses that follow, it seems instead to be associated with the be-

24. For exegesis of the passage, see *KGST*, pp. 50–56.

25. See Schweizer, *Spirit*, pp. 41–50.

26. As Schweizer notes, Luke does not even regard Pentecost as the beginning of the New age, but rather as an intermediate era, "the age of the Church" (Schweizer's term), when all members of the Church are or can be prophets, in fulfillment of the Joel prophecy (*Spirit*, p. 48).

27. Cf. I Cor. 7:26, 29, 31b; 11:26; 15:23 ff., 51 ff.; 16:22. Bultmann to the contrary notwithstanding, the "eschatological existence" of the early Church involved a large measure of anticipation as well as actualization. The Present age had not yet passed away; the time for inheriting the Kingdom had not yet come (I Cor. 2:6; 6:9 f.).

ginning, here on earth, of the final combat with Satan's household. Evidently, it was also understood by Mark (and, perhaps, by Jesus) as a sign of his identity as the Messiah, upon whom the Spirit of God was expected to rest.[28]

However it may have been understood otherwise, the presence of the spirit manifested in prophecy—and also, as we shall see, in exorcism—meant, to those who had ears to hear, that the last days before the Messianic Age had arrived. For the early Church, and also probably for Jesus, the presence of the Spirit was a decisive sign of the times. Afterward, the Kingdom of God would come.

12. JONAH, JOHN, AND JESUS

Various synoptic traditions report that some of Jesus' contemporaries (usually scribes and/or Pharisees) wished him to give a "sign" (semeion) or "sign from heaven." None of these traditions specifies what the sign was supposed to validate. The synoptic Jesus had nowhere declared himself to be the Christ or Messiah. At his trial, not one witness could be found who had heard him make such a claim. It does not seem likely that the scribes would have asked Jesus to prove by a sign something he had never proposed that they believe, that he was the Christ. It is likely, instead, that they wished him to substantiate his proclamation that the Kingdom of God had come near, which was what he had been claiming.

In response to their request, Jesus replied that no sign would be given, except the sign of Jonah. The tradition seems to come from "Q" (Matt. 12:39 = Luke 11:29). Mark reports that Jesus said simply that no sign would be given (Mark 8:11 f.). It is possible that the reference to Jonah is entirely secondary. Or it may be that Mark found it unintelligible and chose to omit it. Both the Matthean and Lukan "explanations" seem forced and secondary. Matt. 12:40 presupposes the death and resurrection tradition. Luke 11:30 refers to some unspecified future activity on the part of the Son of

---

28. Isa. 11:2. In I Sam. 16:13, the Spirit of the Lord came upon David after Samuel anointed him as king. See also *Ps. Sol.* 17:37 and *T. Levi* 18:11. See Schweizer, *Spirit*, p. 11.

man, but does not really fit the context. What the scribes wanted was a sign now.

Such a sign, Jesus implies (Matt. 12:41 = Luke 11:32), is already "here," only "this generation" does not recognize it. Not only Jonah, but in some sense "something greater than Jonah is here." It seems likely that the original version of the saying is as we find it in Matt. 16:4, with no explanation.

But in what way was Jonah a sign to the men of Nineveh? Jonah was the God-sent final preacher of repentance to the ancient Ninevites, proclaiming His impending act of judgment against them on account of their wickedness. The sign to "this generation" is the final preaching of repentance. That was the only sign or clue that the men of Nineveh had—or needed. It is all that "this generation" will get. Even so, for this generation, not only is "Jonah" present in the preaching of repentance, but also "something greater." What could be greater than the preaching of the greatest prophet of the age, albeit the last one who would come, Elijah? In another "Q" saying, Jesus identifies John as not only "prophet" but "more than prophet" (Matt. 11:9), namely Elijah, the greatest (prophet) among those born of women (Matt. 11:11 = Luke 7:28). "Jonah," "something greater than Jonah"; "prophet," "more than prophet."

Perhaps the "sign of Jonah" did not originally even mention Jonah; perhaps it was John whom Jesus named.[29] Or Jesus may have intended to play on the names, a clue in the close similarity between the names Jonah and John (*Yōnāh, Yōhānān*). In any case, it is quite possible that by the "sign of Jonah" he meant to designate John the Baptist, Elijah who must come. To Jesus, himself, John was a sign, namely as Elijah; and those who had ears to hear were to recognize him thus (Matt. 11:7–10 = Luke 7:24–27; Matt. 11:13–15). Elijah was to be a sign to Jesus' contemporaries; he must come first (Mark 9:11). Jesus agreed, and said that Elijah had come (9:12 f.) but that no sign would be given except the "sign of Jonah." That "sign" had apparently been given. Who or what was it? Whether Jesus named John or Jonah, it seems likely that for him, John (Elijah) was this sign. Jesus regarded John's message as

---

29. So also John Creed, *The Gospel According to St. Luke* (London: Macmillan, 1953), pp. 162–63. According to later Jewish lore, Jonah, together with Elisha, had proclaimed the destruction of Jerusalem; see Louis Ginsberg, *The Legends of the Jews* (Philadelphia: Jewish Publication Society, 1913), 4:246 f.

authoritative for his contemporaries: they were to believe him and repent (Matt. 21:32; Mark 11:30 f.). Many, if not "all," people held that John was a real prophet (Mark 11:32). They had evidently understood the "sign" of John—his eschatological significance—even if the scribes and elders had not (Mark 11:33; Luke 7:29 f.). To Jesus, John was Elijah who was to come; to the people, he was perhaps "only" a prophet. But even the appearance of "a real prophet" had, in effect, the same significance; the restoration of prophecy was a mark of the approach of the final time of Judgment and Salvation.

Jonah was the prophet of repentance, par excellence, of the past. In response to his proclamation, the whole of Ninevah had repented and been spared the wrath of Yahweh (Jon. 3:1–10). Elijah was expected as *the* decisive prophet of repentance who was to come at the end of the days of the Old world. The appearance of either Jonah or Elijah would signify the message of repentance, and also the restoration of prophecy to Israel. Both the spirit of prophecy and Elijah were expected at the end of the Present age, but before the "great and terrible day of Yahweh" and the appearance of the Coming age. For Jesus, perhaps, the figures coalesced, their meaning was the same.

At all events, the fact that Elijah–John or Elijah–John–Jonah had come must have been to Jesus, if to no one else, the decisive sign that he and his contemporaries were now living in the last days before the final events were to take place. Both John and Jesus had proclaimed repentance and the nearness of the Kingdom. To ask for further "signs" was out of place—as if God had to offer proof of what he was doing! The "sign" had been given. The people were to repent.

13. EXORCISING DEMONS

Following his baptism by John and temptation "in the wilderness" by Satan, and the arrest of John, Jesus came into Galilee proclaiming that the Kingdom of God had come near and calling for repentance (Mark 1:15). Here his public ministry began. Thereupon he began to summon certain men to follow him, to become "fishers of men"; he preached in the synagogue of Capernaum and cast out or exorcised a demon there. "They" (those in attendance) were amazed both at his teaching with authority (1:22) and the authority with which he commanded the unclean spirits or demons (1:27). As Mark summarized Jesus' preaching in Galilee at 1:15, so he summarized, at 1:39, Jesus' Galilean activity: "And he went throughout all Galilee, preaching in their synagogues and casting out demons."

Mark refers to numerous occasions when Jesus cast out demons; crowds followed him to be healed, which some of the time, if not always, meant that he exorcised their afflicting demons (e.g., 1: 32–34; 3:11 f.). One of the reasons Jesus gathered the Twelve was so that they could join in this work of exorcising demons; they were to be sent out to preach and . . . to cast out demons" (3:14 f.; 6:7), and this is what they reportedly did (6:13). In Mark, Jesus and his disciples are engaged in the work of demon exorcism until the end of the "Galilean ministry" (9:14–29, 38). Demon exorcism is also a central feature of the activity of Jesus and the disciples in the gospels of Matthew and Luke. Besides repeating most of the Markan reports, Matthew and Luke add several other such traditions.[30] But despite the prominence of exorcisms in the synoptic reports, this aspect of Jesus' ministry, and of his disciples' as well, has been given very little attention by New Testament scholars. Often the subject is only referred to incidentally in the context of a general discussion of miracles, or even totally ignored.[31] Not even Schweitzer and Bultmann have much to say about it.[32]

30. Matt. 4:3–10 = Luke 4:3–12 (placed by both Matthew and Luke in the context of the Markan "temptation narrative"); Matt. 12:22 f. = Luke 11:14 and Matt. 12:27 f. = Luke 11:18b–20 (placed again by both Matthew and Luke in the same Markan setting, here the Beelzebul controversy); cf. Matt. 11:18b = Luke 7:33b; Matt. 4:24 = Luke 6:18 f.; Matt. 12:43–45 = Luke 11:24–26; Luke 7:21; 8:2; 10:17–20 (cf. Matt. 16:19; 18:18); Luke 13:10–17.

31. E.g., Günther Bornkamm, Jesus of Nazareth (London: Hodder & Stoughton, 1960), pp. 130 ff.; Eduard Schweizer, Jesus (Richmond: John Knox Press, 1971), pp. 43–45. C. H. Dodd does not discuss exorcism in his new book on Jesus, The Founder of Christianity (New York: Macmillan, 1970).

32. The following are among the more important treatments of the subject. On Jewish background: Billerbeck 1:136–49, 983–84; 4:501–35; Paul Volz, Die Eschatologie der jüdischen Gemeinde, 2d ed. (Tübingen: J. C. B. Mohr, 1934), pp. 8 ff., 68, 83–89. On the Markan and New Testament background: Grundmann, Der Begriff, pp. 47–55; James M. Robinson, The Problem of History in Mark, SBT no. 21 (London: SCM, 1957); Howard C. Kee, "The Terminology of Mark's Exorcism Stories," NTS 14 (1968):232–46. On

Since the substance of Jesus' message was, in effect, "Repent, the Kingdom of God has come near," and the two tasks which he was characteristically engaged in carrying out were the proclamation of this message and the exorcism of demons, it might reasonably be expected that his exorcism of demons had something to do with his belief that the Kingdom of God had come near. This connection appears implicitly in the work he assigns to his disciples or "apostles"; he sends them forth to cast out demons and proclaim that the Kingdom of God has come near.[33]

In the case of the mission of the apostles, there is no doubt as to the nature of the relationship between demon exorcising and the coming of the Kingdom of God. The former, like the preaching of repentance, was preliminary and preparatory to the coming of the Kingdom. The missionaries were to exorcise demons and proclaim that the Kingdom had come near.[34] They were sent out because "the harvest is plentiful, but the laborers are few" (Matt. 9:37 = Luke 10:2), to extend Jesus' own work of proclamation and exorcism in order to reach as many persons as possible before the parousia. Jesus urges the apostles to travel light and make haste.[35] They "will not have gone through all the towns of Israel before the Son of man comes" (Matt. 10:23).

The saying at Matt. 12:28 (=Luke 11:20), however, has suggested to many interpreters a different connection between demon exorcism and the proclamation of the Kingdom: "But if it is by the Spirit of God that I cast out demons, then the Kingdom of God *ephthasen eph' humas.*" The possible ambiguity of the Greek expression is adequately conveyed in the RSV translation "has come upon you." Does this mean that the Kingdom has arrived, or, as in the several instances where the verb *engizein* appears, that it is, or has come, near? If the former, exorcisms should signify the presence

---

Jesus' understanding of Satan and the demons: Weiss, *Jesus' Proclamation*, pp. 74–81; Weiss, *Predigt* (1900), pp. 26–27, 230–35; Vincent Taylor, *The Gospel According to St. Mark* (London: Macmillan, 1955), pp. 237–44; Manson, *Jesus and the Christian*, pp. 77–88; Otto Betz, "Jesu heiliger Krieg," *NT* 2 (1958):117 ff. See also *KGST*, pp. 30–56.

33. Matt. 10:1, 7; Luke 9:1 f.; 10:9, 11, 17, 19. The number seventy or seventy-two in Luke 10 is probably secondary (see sec. 14n41 of this study), but the "instructions" in Luke 10 otherwise correspond to those in Matt. 10 and Luke 9, and are probably from Q.

34. *Engiken eph' humas hē basileia tou theou:* Matt. 10:7 f.; Luke 10:9, 11; cf. Matt. 10:1; Luke 9:1 f.; Luke 10:17, 19.

35. Matt. 10:9–14 and parallels.

of the Kingdom. Thus, a number of interpreters describe the exorcisms as "signs" of the presence or "dawning" of the Kingdom, or as manifestations of its "powers."[36] But exorcisms are nowhere designated as "signs" in the synoptic tradition, nor is there any reference to the "powers" or "power" of the Kingdom of God.[37] Jesus probably did not speak Greek, and we do not know what Aramaic (or Hebrew) expression he may have actually used in the case of this particular saying. Elsewhere, both Matthew and Luke consistently seem to have understood that Jesus looked for the coming of the Kingdom in the future. It may be that, in this one instance, they report a saying that had a different meaning, though neither suggests that the saying is problematic as far as his own sense of its meaning is concerned; in the same context, Matthew presents a saying which makes it clear that the Age to come has not yet come (12:32).[38] It would seem more likely that the sense here, as is clearly the case with Jesus' instructions to the Apostles (Matt. 10; Luke 9, 10) is that exorcism, like preaching, is preparatory to the coming of the Kingdom of God.

This sense becomes more evident when we consider the context in which the saying appears, the so-called Beelzebul controversy (Mark 3:22–30). It is to be recalled that Satan was "the prince of demons," the one who, it is indicated at the outset of Jesus' ministry, has possession of all the kingdoms of the world (Matt. 4:8 f. = Luke 4:5–7). By afflicting people, causing misery through his demons, he holds people in bondage, trying to corrupt the faithful.[39] The intertestamental literature and the Dead Sea Scrolls make it plain that, in various Jewish circles during the first century AD (and the last one or two BC), it was understood that Satan had been given—or had seized—control of the earth. From this standpoint, it is obvious that, so long as Satan rules on earth, the Kingdom of God has not yet been established here.

In Jesus' response to the "scribes," he asks, "How can Satan cast out Satan?" (Mark 3:23). The demon or demons exorcised are referred to here, and also at 3:26, as "Satan." Satan works through his demons. The demons represent Satan. "But no one can enter a

36. E.g., Keck, A Future, pp. 126, 246.
37. Cf. Mark 9:1, where the coming of the Kingdom with power is clearly indicated as a future event.
38. The terms "Kingdom of God" and "Age to come" are used interchangeably at Mark 10:23, 25, 30 = Luke 18:24 f., 29 f.
39. E.g., Mark 4:15 and parallels; Luke 13:10–16.

strong man's house and plunder his goods, unless he first binds the strong man; then indeed he may plunder his house" (Mark 3:27). What does this mean? If we are to understand that the strong man = Satan, and that Jesus had already bound him, then we might see the exorcisms in terms of plundering his goods, "mopping up" after victory. But Satan also represents the demons, and vice versa; moreover, there is no indication here or elsewhere that Satan had already been bound. The more likely meaning, then, is that by his exorcisms, Jesus is binding the demons, and thus also Satan himself. The "goods" being plundered are those persons who previously had been afflicted, and now are loosed or freed from their afflictions and for the Kingdom of God. It may also be implicit here that the defeat of the demons spells the ultimate doom of Satan's rule or kingdom.[40]

In that case, the connection between Jesus' exorcisms and his proclamation about the Kingdom of God at Matt. 12:28 = Luke 11:20 becomes clear. If it is by the power (or spirit) of God that Jesus is overpowering the demons (rather than, as his opponents allege, by Satan's own power), his victories signify that Satan is being bound. In the process, the way is being cleared for the establishment of God's rule on earth. The defeat of the demons means, to those who understand what is happening, that the time for the establishment of God's Kingdom has come near. This also is the apparent implication of the saying at Luke 10:17–20. Jesus had given his apostles authority over the demons. They return from their urgent mission, jubilant over their success. Their victories prompt Jesus to experience or report a prophetic vision of Satan's final defeat: "And he said to them, 'I saw Satan fall like lightning from heaven'" (10:18).

The Kingdom of God would soon be established on earth. In the meantime, by casting out demons, Jesus and his followers were freeing men, women, and children from the power of Satan and

40. Thus also Reginald H. Fuller, *The Mission and Achievement of Jesus,* SBT no. 12 (London: SCM, 1963), p. 38. Such, perhaps, is the meaning of Matt. 11:12: "From the days of John the Baptist until now, the kingdom of heaven has been coming violently, and men of violence take it by force." Jesus' ministry of preaching and exorcism began shortly after the arrest of John. There is no record that John exorcised demons, but Jesus and his followers did. The exorcisms began after the days of John. Were Jesus and his followers the "men of violence"? They were overpowering Satan's forces, the demons, with violence, preparing for the establishment of the Kingdom of God on earth. Thus, the demons' complaint, Mark 1:24.

making them ready for the coming of the Kingdom of God. At the same time, by overcoming or binding the power of Satan, they were preparing for the final establishment by God of his Kingdom or rule on earth. When that happened, there would be no more place on earth for Satan and his demons.

14. THE MISSION OF THE TWELVE AND THE BANQUET IN THE WILDERNESS

At some point, late in his ministry in Galilee according to the synoptic tradition, Jesus, his disciples, and a "great throng" of other followers converged upon a lonely place or desert (Mark 6:30–46 and parallels; 8:1–10 = Matt. 15:32–39). For a while Jesus taught them (6:34) and healed those who were sick (in Matthew and Luke only). Then—in the story of the 4,000, after three days— the disciples urged Jesus to send the crowd away to buy themselves food. But Jesus told them to offer their own few provisions to the crowd, whom he then instructed to be seated; then he "looked up to heaven," blessed the bread, and, through the disciples, distributed fragments of bread and fish to all the people. After they had eaten, he dismissed the crowd and went off by himself to pray.

The episode was evidently enigmatic to the evangelists, and has been to subsequent interpreters as well. As it stands, it has been, in part, made over into a miracle story, probably under the influence of II Kings 4:42–44. Mark hints at some esoteric numerological significance in a later pericope (8:14–21) based on the catchword "leaven."[41] Matthew apparently rejects this interpretation (16:11 f.) and Luke omits it, along with the whole episode of the 4,000. Various writers have noted certain sacramental aspects: Jesus

41. It is conceivable that Mark understood the figure twelve to represent the mission to Israel, and seven the mission to the Gentiles. Jewish-Christian tradition posited twelve "tribes" of Israel, and seventy Gentile (non-Jewish) "nations." Seven comprises the number of the Gentile churches in Rev. 1–3. Luke uses the figures seven (Acts 6) and seventy (Luke 10) to represent Gentile Christianity. Mark has two meals in the wilderness; Luke has two missions, but omits the second meal in which seven baskets are left over. In each case, the twelve ("Jew") are first, then the seven or seventy ("Greek"— cf. Rom. 2:10). The image of baskets full of crumbs may have been meant to suggest that only a "remnant" would be saved (cf. Matt. 7:13 f., 22 f.; Rom. 9:27).

blesses the bread, breaks it (and cuts the fish), and gives the pieces (through his disciples) to the people, whom he afterwards dismisses. It may be significant that the Eucharist or Last Supper is regularly represented in early Christian catacomb art—and even in da Vinci's famous painting—by bread *and* fish. Jesus, and possibly his disciples, may have understood the wilderness banquet sacramentally, but that meaning was, perhaps, lost or subordinated in the time of the evangelists, who report the incident(s) as a miracle story.

If there is a historical basis for the report, reworked as it may be, can we discern anything of its significance for Jesus and those present? What would Jesus and his followers, together with a crowd of four or five thousand, have been doing in the wilderness? Why had the crowd neglected to bring their own food? What did Jesus teach them there? What did he intend to do for them by distributing the fragments of food?

It cannot be assumed that Mark (or the other evangelists) provide an accurate chronology of events and conversations. Neither, however, can it be assumed that the various pericopes were inevitably dislocated from their original settings. It may be significant that the feeding in the wilderness enjoys a certain coherence in its Markan context, which appears also, to a lesser extent, in the Matthean and Lukan accounts.

As early as Mark 1:17, the role of Jesus' followers is defined: they are to cease fishing for fish and become "fishers of men." C. W. F. Smith has called attention to the eschatological meaning of this designation, maintaining that it refers to the task of gathering the people for judgment.[42] It may also mean gathering those who are to participate in the Age to come. In Matt. 13:47, Jesus declares that, at the Judgment, the righteous "fish" will enter the Kingdom of heaven, the evil ones will be assigned to perdition.

Following Mark 1:17, Jesus' own activity as exorcist and healer is reported (along with some other traditions); then, in 3:13 ff., the number of "apostles," twelve, is completed. They are "to be with him [for a while] and [later] to be sent out to preach and have authority to cast out demons" (cf. Luke 10:19). Their function, then, is to extend Jesus' own ministry of preaching and exorcism, tasks which, as we have seen, were understood as preliminary and preparatory to the coming of the Kingdom of God.

42. "Fishers of Men," *JBL* 78 (1959):187–203.

After recording various other traditions, Mark reports that Jesus then did send out the Twelve to preach repentance, exorcise, and heal (6:7–13). That they also proclaimed the nearness of the Kingdom of God we learn, explicitly, from "Q" traditions (Matt. 9:35—10:15; Luke 9:1–5; cf. 10:1–12). Despite the wishes of some interpreters, it is to be noted that these "particular instructions apply literally only to this brief mission during Jesus' lifetime."[43] There is no reason to suppose that Matt. 10:23 misrepresents Jesus' understanding of the urgency of their mission.[44] Nor is there reason to suppose that the "apostles" neglected their task of exorcising and preaching repentance in the face of the imminence of Judgment and the Kingdom. Mark and Luke indicate that they completed their mission and returned to Jesus, reporting "all that they had done and taught" (Mark 6:30; Luke 9:10; cf. 10:17). Matthew does not report their return, but implies that they have rejoined Jesus by the beginning of chapter 12, probably because Matthew needed "the disciples" present to prompt the Pharisees' complaint in 12:1 ff. and the "explanation" of the parables (13:10), notably of the parable of the weeds in 13:36 ff. Consequently, Matthew has Jesus withdraw to the "lonely place" upon hearing of the fate of the Baptist rather than upon the return of the disciples (14:12 f.).

That a great crowd should have followed upon the heels of the missionary Apostles is not surprising. Had they not been proclaiming, on Jesus' authority, that the Kingdom of God was near and validating this message by their exorcisms? Those who took this message seriously would certainly have wished to see the one who had sent the messengers, and to be near him when the Kingdom came. Contrary to the impression given in Matthew (14:14; 15:30 f.), Mark does not say that the crowds came in order to be healed—as if the Apostles had been unable to heal them (cf. Luke 10:17 f.)—but because many of the crowd "knew them" (6:33) and wanted to be with them. According to Mark, Jesus taught them, but no mention is made of healing.[45] Luke adds that he taught them about the Kingdom of God. What he taught them about the Kingdom of God we do not know, but not long before, he had sent out the Twelve to proclaim its nearness. He had expected it to come before they returned from completing their mission (Matt.

43. Cranfield, St. Mark, p. 200.
44. See KGST, pp. 66–71.
45. Cf. Mark 10:1b = Matt. 19:2; Matt. 21:14 f.

10:23). The crowd, we can infer, came to Jesus prompted by the "apostles'" announcement that the Kingdom was near. They had left homes and family and were now eager to know more about the Kingdom of God, if not indeed to be present for its actualization. Such, then, seems to have been the context in which Jesus proceeded to "feed" the multitude.

Against this background, the sacramental character of the feeding becomes more significant. As in the case of the Last Supper, Jesus apparently acted out in advance, with the other participants, a celebration of the Messianic Banquet, a prominent feature of the life of blessedness in the Kingdom of God (e.g., Matt. 8:11 f.; Luke 13:28 f.; 14:15 ff.). At the Last Supper, he vowed that he would (eat and) drink with his followers—in the Kingdom of God (Mark 14:25; cf. Luke 22:16-18). The early Church celebrated the Eucharist in expectation that the Messiah would soon come; this hope was connected in some way or other with the supper.[46]

What connection Jesus may have seen between the "meal" in the wilderness and the coming of the Kingdom does not appear in the tradition as we have it. Schweitzer proposed that Jesus was consecrating the communicants, setting them apart as those who could thereby be assured of inclusion in the coming Kingdom. In this case, the significance of the meal would have been similar to that of the baptism performed by John, who also had consecrated a great crowd in the wilderness, preparatory to the coming of the Kingdom of God (Matt. 3:1 ff.). It has also been suggested that Jesus here was celebrating the messianic meal "proleptically" with his followers. In those days Jesus and his followers were praying and longing for the coming of the Kingdom of God (Matt. 6:10, 33, and parallels; Luke 12:32 ff.). Jesus had expected it to arrive before his "apostles" could complete their work (Matt. 10:23). But it had not come. Could it be that Jesus attempted to induce the coming of the Kingdom through participatory or "sympathetic magic"? By acting out the presence of the Kingdom, God might be moved to let it come. Jesus and his followers did not adopt a passive attitude about the coming of the Kingdom. The central theme in the "Lord's Prayer" was the petition for the coming of the King-

---

46. See secs. 24 and 27 of this study. Against G. H. Boobyer, B. van Iersel argues effectively for the view that the meal was understood in a eucharistic sense by the early Church and the evangelists: "Die wunderbare Speisung und das Abendmahl in der synoptischen Tradition," *NT* 7 (1964):167–94.

dom (Matt. 6:10=Luke 11:2). By praying, Jesus evidently believed that God might be prevailed on to send His Kingdom sooner than otherwise (so also Luke 18:1–8), or to bring it without first bringing the time to tribulation (so also Mark 14:32–39).

Also imbedded in the "Lord's Prayer" is the petition "Give us our bread for tomorrow today" (Matt. 6:11; cf. Luke 11:3). The prayer otherwise has to do entirely with the coming of the Messianic Age: v. 10, "Thy [God's] Kingdom come"; v. 12, "Forgive us our offenses" (in preparation for its coming, so that we may be permitted to enter it when it comes); v. 13, "spare us the final tribulation of the Evil One" (i.e., bring the Kingdom without making us first have to suffer the otherwise ordained "woes," here probably connected with Satan's anticipated final effort to retain his power on earth; cf. Rev. 12:12).

What does a petition about bread have to do with the coming of the Kingdom of God? The later sayings "on anxiety" express confidence that God will provide food, drink, and clothing for the faithful (Matt. 6:25–34 and parallels). It is possible that Jesus meant that his followers should, nevertheless, pray that God would supply them with "daily" bread "each day" during the interim until the arrival of the Kingdom. This, probably, was Luke's understanding, for Luke reads *kath' hemeran* (each day) instead of Matthew's *semeron* (today). Elsewhere, however, Luke had adjusted tradition, either in accordance with his awareness that the Kingdom had not come during Jesus' lifetime[47] or to provide a "better," i.e., less problematic, reading. It is likely that here Matthew's version is closer to the original. In any case, the key word is the adjective *epiousion*, rendered by the RSV editors, no doubt with some misgiving, as "daily." Literally, it means "for tomorrow," "for the day to come." To translate it as "daily" expresses a certain redundancy otherwise uncharacteristic of Jesus' sayings: "Give us each day our daily bread." What other kind of bread might one desire "this day" or any day?

But if "for tomorrow" is read, what can it mean? Why would one pray to receive today the bread for tomorrow? Should one be anxious for tomorrow after all (Matt. 6:34)? It is this seemingly logical difficulty that has led interpreters to prefer the redundant,

47. E.g., Luke 19:11; Acts 1:7; his adjustment of the saying at Mark 14:62 = Luke 22:69; and his omission of the sayings at Mark 1:15 and Matt. 10:23.

if inaccurate, reading, "daily." For instance, one writes, "It is not to be expected that in the same breath one should utter what makes an absurd or incongruous first impression."[48] Such a petition is incongruous, however, only if one neglects to take into account Jesus' eschatological outlook. When this is recognized, the meaning is parallel to that of the first petition: "Thy Kingdom come [soon]"; "Give us the bread of the messianic banquet [i.e., the Kingdom of God] today."[49] That bread would be eaten in the Kingdom of God is taken for granted (Luke 14:15; cf. Deut. 8:9a). Moreover, there would be *two* "fish" for food in those days: the two great sea monsters, Behemoth and Leviathan.[50]

Was it in Jesus' mind that God might bring His Kingdom on that day when he celebrated, proleptically or symbolically, the messianic feast with his followers in the wilderness?[51] He had, just recently, sent out the Twelve to proclaim its nearness, as "laborers for the harvest," expecting the Son of man to appear before they returned. Would this celebration in the wilderness set in motion the final pattern of eschatological events that would culminate in the establishment of God's Kingdom on earth? While blessing the bread, Jesus "looked up to heaven." Was he expecting the Kingdom—or Son of man—to appear? Perhaps he was only looking to the place of God's abode. At the end of the observance, the Kingdom not having come, Jesus dismissed the crowd, took leave of his disciples, and withdrew to pray (Mark 6:45 f.). The only other occasion

48. Lemuel S. Potwin, " 'Epiousios,' " JBL 12 (1893):17.

49. See Reumann, Jesus, pp. 104–5: "What ought to astonish us is that Jesus taught his disciples to pray for such 'bread'—which his Jewish contemporaries expected only in the 'last times'— here and now, in the present, 'this day.' " Parallelism or repetition of thought but in different terms is the central feature of Hebrew poetic form. Such parallelism also appears at the end of the "Lord's Prayer": "Lead us not into Temptation / [But] Deliver us from the Evil One." If, as Reumann and others propose, the Matthean statement "Thy will be done, on earth as it is in heaven" was contributed by that evangelist, the original parallelism in the prayer would have been, as in Luke 11:2 f., "Thy Kingdom come. / Give us today our bread for the morrow."

50. Syr. Baruch 29:3 f. See Erwin R. Goodenough's discussion of the Jewish fish meal he believes was practiced in anticipation of the Messianic age: Jewish Symbols in the Greco-Roman Period (New York: Pantheon, 1952), 5:31–61.

51. The Old Testament prophets not only proclaimed but sometimes acted out symbolically events to come, e.g., Jer. 32:9; Ezek. 4:1 ff. Cf. Dodd, The Founder, p. 133: "Jesus made use of the image of a feast to signify the blessings of the kingdom of God consummated in a world beyond this." Dodd proposes that Jesus intended the meal with the five thousand as an "acted parable," after the pattern of earlier Hebrew prophets.

on which Jesus himself withdraws and prays (in the synoptic tradition) is at Gethsemane (Mark 14:32–36). Here, his prayer has in effect the substance of that which he urges upon Peter, that even at this late hour the Kingdom might come without the necessity of his (or their) suffering "temptation" (*peirasmos*, Mark 14:38; cf. Matt. 6:13=Luke 11:4c). The central theme in his followers' prayers also was to be that God would bring his Kingdom. It is not unreasonable to assume that Jesus withdrew following the feeding in the wilderness, himself to pray for the coming of the Kingdom.

The Kingdom did not then come, though two of the evangelists apparently thought it appropriate to record immediately afterwards a vision of Jesus as the exalted or supernatural Messiah "walking on water" (Mark 6:47–52=Matt. 14:24–33), as if to show that the messianic hope would, ultimately, be fulfilled, and to reassure later Christians that Jesus was, or would be, the Messiah, even though he had not yet come as such.

Jesus and some of his followers may have continued to hope that the Kingdom of God might come in connection with their pre-enactment of the Messianic Banquet. It is usually assumed that the two meals—the "feeding" of the five thousand and of the four thousand—reported in Mark and Matthew are to be understood as duplicate versions of the same event. Reworked from the standpoint of later interests as they may be, however, could it be that these "duplicate" reports reflect a recollection that Jesus had celebrated more than one such sacramental and anticipatory meal with his followers? At any rate, the Last Supper, though different in certain respects, was another such meal.

Perhaps Schweitzer was correct: the fact that the Twelve returned from their mission through Israel without the dawning of the parousia (cf. Matt. 10:23) led Jesus to conclude that he, himself, must bear the "tribulation" before it could come. Or, conceivably, it was the fact that it did not come when he "fed" the multitudes who had gathered in response to the announcement by the Twelve that it was near, which occasioned his determination to go then to Jerusalem. The first of the "passion predictions" follows closely upon the "feeding" of the "4,000" in Mark and Matthew. Or it may be that Jesus was content, as later in his prayer at Gethsemane, to let God's will be done and to wait until another time for Him to bring His Kingdom. In any case, as the tradition tells it, Jesus shortly afterward set out for Jerusalem.

IV

To Jerusalem

SINCE THE DAYS of Amos, it had been understood that
God ruled from Zion (Jerusalem) (Amos 1:2). This
was the place where the Lord's anointed had dwelt of old, from
the days of David to Zerubbabel and Joshua the High Priest and
the later Maccabaean "kings." There kings were to be crowned
(Ps. 2:6). In the later literature, it was the place where God would
manifest himself in the Messianic Age (Joel 3:16 ff.; Zech. 14:4 f.,
9).

Despite the mission and message to the towns of Galilee, the
Kingdom had not come. A series of episodes and sayings indicates
that Jesus came to believe, if he had not done so before, that the
Kingdom of God would in some way or other be inaugurated by or
with his activity in Jerusalem. This chapter sketches the basic pattern indicated in these several traditions. It should be noted that
the suggested interpretation of these several events does not pre-
suppose any particular chronological sequence. As a convenience,
they are taken up in the order in which Mark presents them, but
in any order, their eschatological (if not also messianic) character
would be equally evident.

15. "FOLLOW ME"

Simon and Andrew had left their nets and followed Jesus (Mark
1:18). With others of the Twelve, they had been sent out on their
flying mission, exorcising and preaching through the villages or
towns of "Israel" (Matt. 10:6, 23). It may be that this was not to
include the villages of Judea also. According to Matthew, they
were to avoid the towns of Samaria. It would have been difficult to

71

reach Judea without going through Samaria. They did not, apparently, include Jerusalem on their missionary itinerary.[1] We do not know the exact number of towns or villages in Galilee and Judea in those days.[2] But six pairs of "Apostles," traveling rapidly, probably could have completed the mission in a few weeks. They were reportedly tired upon their return (Mark 6:31). Jesus may have hoped that the Kingdom of God would come while he and his disciples remained in the North. Possibly a trace of this expectation appears in the tradition that Jesus, as risen (?) Messiah, would "go before," i.e., lead, his followers to Galilee.[3] But the Kingdom did not come in Galilee.

The whole episode at Caesarea Philippi and the various passion predictions following it are highly problematic. But it is generally evident, especially in Mark, that afterward Jesus began his movement, with his disciples and other followers, toward Jerusalem. Previously Jesus had called his disciples to "follow" him. Their work, like his own, had been to cast out demons and proclaim repentance and the nearness of the Kingdom. They had been "fishers of men," "laborers for the harvest" (Matt. 9:37 f. = Luke 10:2), preparing Israel, or at least Galileans, for the coming of the Kingdom. Crowds had begun to follow Jesus, inspired by his and his disciples' proclamation and activity, even into the wilderness by the Sea of Galilee, looking for the Kingdom of God to come. Now Jesus turned toward Jerusalem. Those who wished to enter the Kingdom were now summoned to follow him to Jerusalem.

Immediately after the first passion prediction (Mark 8:31–33), Jesus called "the multitude" as well as his disciples to "follow me" if they wished to save their lives (8:34 f.). That the meaning is eschatological is obvious in the reference to the coming of the Son of man in glory with angels, and coming of the Kingdom which (some of) those present would live to see.[4] By itself, this summons

1. Mark seems to imply that Jesus and his followers by-passed Samaria on their way to Jerusalem, going instead through Perea (10:1).
2. *The Westminster Historical Atlas to the Bible,* eds. G. E. Wright and F. V. Filson, rev. ed. (Philadelphia: Westminster, 1956), p. 90, shows thirteen sites in Galilee, twelve in Judea, and only fifty in all of Palestine during the time of Jesus.
3. Mark 14:28; 16:7 and the Matthean parallels; also Matt. 28:10, 16. The fact that this expectation was not actualized favors its historicity. See J. Weiss, *Primitive Christianity* (New York: Harper, 1959), 1:14–18; and C. F. Evans, "I Will Go before You into Galilee," *JTS* 5 (n.s., 1954):3–18.
4. Mark 8:38; 9:1. The limitation to "some" of those present may reflect

to follow would not be especially noteworthy. But there are other such invitations on the way to Jerusalem.

The rich "young" man is not only to sell all that he has and give the proceeds to the poor; he is to follow Jesus (Mark 10:21) if he wishes to enter the Kingdom of God. In contrast, Peter and the others who are assured of participation in the Kingdom have left house and family and followed Jesus (10:28 f.). We must avoid allegorizing or spiritualizing the idea of "following," as if it meant following Jesus' teaching or example. Mark describes the procession toward Jerusalem, Jesus walking ahead, the others literally following (10:32). The crowd which had been following him from Galilee and Perea (Mark 10:1 = Matt. 19:1 f.) comes along after him, possibly joined by new followers as he leaves Jericho for Jerusalem (Mark 10:46 = Matt. 20:29). Upon being healed, Bartimaeus, who somehow had come under the impression that Jesus was the Messiah, "followed him on the way" to Jerusalem (Mark 10:52).

The "Galilean pilgrims"—a group of companions more numerous than the "Twelve"—who accompany Jesus on his way from the Mount of Olives to Jerusalem, some running ahead, others following, hail Jesus as "the Coming One" and look for the coming of the Kingdom of David, if not the Kingdom of God.[5] A "multitude" accompanies Jesus as he "cleanses" the Temple, their presence preventing the authorities from apprehending him there (Mark 11:18, 32; 12:12). So many followers remained with Jesus that it was only "by stealth" (14:1 f.) that the authorities could arrest and "try" him. Even at the cross, though present only "from afar," there were "many women" who had followed him from Galilee. After his death, Joseph of Arimathea, whom Matthew describes as one of his followers, was "also looking for the Kingdom of God" (Mark 15:43).

Jesus' followers who expected that the Kingdom would come were disappointed. It did not come in Jerusalem. Afterward, perhaps some of them returned to Galilee to look for its coming and

Mark's awareness (c. 60–70 AD) that most of Jesus' contemporaries had died by this time. So also Erich Grässer, *Das Problem der Parusieverzögerung in den synoptischen Evangelien und in der Apostelgeschichte,* 2d ed. (Berlin: Töpelmann, 1960), esp. pp. 128 ff. The reference to "cross" in Mark 8:34 is also evidently a Christianization.

5. See sec. 18 of this study.

the coming of Jesus as the Messiah. Others remained in Jerusalem
(Acts 1–8). All, apparently, continued to look for the coming of
the Kingdom of God.[6]

16. THE REQUEST OF THE BROTHERS (MARK 10:35–45)

After both the second and the third "passion predictions" (Mark
9:31 f., 10:33 f.), which are set in the context of the journey to
Jerusalem, Jesus' disciples reportedly were arguing among themselves as to which was (or was to be) the greatest. Quite possibly
Mark gives duplicate or parallel recensions of the same occasion.
The situations in both cases are similar. As the earlier version
stands (9:33–35), it may reflect a criticism of claims by adherents
of one or another of the "Apostles" to primacy during the days of
the early Church.[7] There is, however, a connection between Jesus'
predictions about events to take place in Jerusalem and the disciples' discussion as to which of them would be foremost. Moreover, the authenticity of the tradition is attested by the pretentious
nature of their aspirations which was noted not only by Jesus,
but was also an embarrassment to the later evangelists. Matthew
transfers the request on behalf of the sons of Zebedee to the lips
of their mother; Luke omits it altogether.

One might suppose, though it would scarcely do honor to the
Apostles, that the reason for their concern as to which one of them
would be first was occasioned by their literal acceptance of Jesus'
passion announcement. Jesus was to die. When he was gone, who
would be in charge? Such a supposition does not take into account
the expectation that the Kingdom of God was coming. The real
question in the minds of the disciples was which of them would
have the highest rank in the Kingdom of God. This is obviously
the meaning of the request of the sons of Zebedee. When Jesus
is enthroned as Son of man or Messiah, they wish to sit at his
right hand and his left. If they were not so brash as to visualize a

6. See sec. 27 of this study.
7. Peter and "the beloved disciple," presumably John, are accorded special prominence in other Gospels. James, the brother of Jesus, was also one of
the so-called pillars, in fact, evidently the primate of the Jerusalem Church,
though Paul scarcely granted him deference as such (Gal. 1:18 f.; 2:6–9).

triumvirate, they at least wished to be vice-regents, or Prime Minister and Secretary of State.

Something of the sort is evidently at the root of the more general discussion in Mark 9:33 ff. Matthew sees the meaning of their concern to be "Who is [to be] greatest in the Kingdom of heaven?" (Matt. 18:1). Both in Mark and Matthew (and in other versions), Jesus indicates a child or servant as the model for those who aspire to greatness in the Kingdom of God.[8] The number and diversity of these sayings indicates that the early Christians had trouble interpreting his meaning.[9] But the meaning of Mark 10:42–44 is unmistakable: those who wish to be great in the court of the Messiah must now be servant or slave. The saying at 9:35 is to the same effect: one who would be first must now become servant (*diakonos*). The next verse reports that Jesus took a *pais* to illustrate his point. It is customary, here, to translate *pais* as "child." But it may also mean "servant" or "slave,"[10] and is principally used in the Septuagint for *'ebed*, "servant." The context here suggests that Jesus took a servant or slave, perhaps a young servant or slave. His point was that, if one aspired to greatness in the Kingdom, he must now become as servant; it was not a general statement about children and their innocence or humility. The meaning proposed here accords with Jesus' general view that the Kingdom would be inherited by the poor, the *am-ha aretz*, the "sinners," the low-caste and unpretentious, that the last would be first.[11]

It is significant that Jesus does not take issue with the brothers' assumption that there would be special seats of honor and office in the coming Kingdom. He says only that he does not have authority to grant these distinctions (Mark 10:40), and that those who aspire to them must qualify by service now (cf. Matt. 5:3–10). Jesus did not seem to doubt that at the Judgment (or in the

---

8. Luke 9:46–48; 18:17; Mark 10:15; 10:43 f. and parallels. See sec. 6n52. However, see Schweitzer, *Kingdom of God*, p. 96: "To Jesus the young children of the final human generation are destined to enter the Kingdom as they are. . . . The Kingdom will have come before they are grown up."

9. The saying at Mark 10:15 and parallels may represent another question, as indicated in the context, viz., the criteria for entering the Kingdom, not who is to be greatest there. Matthew seems to conflate the two (18:3 f.).

10. Walter Bauer, *A Greek-English Lexicon of the New Testament*, eds. W. F. Arndt and F. W. Gingrich (Chicago: University of Chicago Press, 1957), p. 609.

11. See my article "Friends by Unrighteous Mammon," and above, pp. 33–34.

Kingdom of God?) he would occupy the central throne, or that some or all twelve of the others might share rule with him there (so also Matt. 19:28=Luke 22:30).

Is it only a coincidence that this discussion took place on the way to Jerusalem? Or is it because Jesus and his disciples were expecting the Kingdom of God to begin at the end of their journey to the Holy City?

17. THE REQUEST OF BARTIMAEUS

It would be of interest to know whether the son of Timaeus had heard that Jesus of Nazareth was the "Son of David" from the disciples and/or the "great multitude" traveling past him as he sat by the roadside, or whether he drew his own conclusions from what he heard.[12] As Mark tells the story, many (presumably from the great multitude accompanying Jesus) warned (*epitimōn*) Bartimaeus to be quiet (10:48). The verb *epitiman* is common in exorcism scenes, where it may originally have been part of a formula used to overpower the demons, but it seems to have been understood by Mark as an admonition to keep the divine or Messianic identity of Jesus secret.[13] But Jesus himself did not "rebuke" Bartimaeus. Instead, he summoned him and asked, "What do you want me to do for you?" (10:51). Instead of telling Bartimaeus to be quiet, Jesus evidently perceived Bartimaeus' outcry as an expression of faith (10:52). After Bartimaeus was healed, Jesus did not "charge" him to say nothing, but told him simply to go his way.

Either Jesus or Mark seems to have abandoned any reticence about disclosing—or acknowledging—publicly Jesus' messianic identity. ("Son of David" here is probably a messianic title, equivalent to "Messiah" or "Christ.") Is it only coincidence that here, for the first time, on the final "leg" of the journey to Jerusalem, Jesus inspired and acknowledged public identification of himself as the Messiah? Did he expect soon to be disclosed as such?

Bartimaeus had received his sight. Healed and also believing,

12. See the excellent discussion of the Bartimaeus episode by Charles W. F. Smith, *The Paradox of Jesus in the Gospels* (Philadelphia: Westminster, 1969), pp. 135–44.
13. Cf. Mark 1:25; 3:12: 8:30. See Kee, "Terminology."

he was now ready for the Kingdom of God. Why did he join the multitude who followed Jesus to Jerusalem? Did he expect something more important than the restoration of his sight to happen there? Soon the same crowd, presumably including Bartimaeus, would be cheering Jesus as "the Coming One" (*ho erchomenos*) of God and praising Him for the coming Messianic Kingdom (Mark 11:9 f.).

18. THE ENTRY INTO JERUSALEM (MARK 11:1–10)

The Mount of Olives.—Upon arriving at the Mount of Olives, Jesus sent two of his disciples to procure a special colt or ass, whose messianic significance will be noted shortly. Evidently, as Luke reports (19:37), it was from the Mount of Olives that Jesus, the same day, proceeded to Jerusalem, accompanied by the throng shouting their joy or prayers for the coming Messiah and/or Messianic Age.

It could be, of course, that the Mount of Olives was simply the place where Jesus happened to make his camp while visiting Jerusalem for the Passover. It was a convenient distance from Jerusalem (Acts 1:12). It was also, at least to some Jews, a place of messianic importance.[14] It was the highest location in the vicinity of Jerusalem. If the Messiah or Son of man was expected to descend from heaven to earth, it could be expected that he would first touch earth here. According to Zech. 14:4, God Himself would stand on the Mount of Olives "on that day," i.e., the day when the Messianic Age was to begin.

It is possible that Jesus' saying about prayer for the moving of "this mountain" (Mark 11:23) assumes the validity of this expectation (Zech. 14:4–10). On "that day" the Mount of Olives was to be split in two, part of it moving to the North, another part to the South, opening a wide plain around Jerusalem. Then God will come (to Jerusalem), nature will be transformed, and the Kingdom of God will be established over all the earth (14:5c–9). Mark 11:25 contains this evangelist's only reminiscence of the "Lord's Prayer." Perhaps the tradition about praying for the moving of "this mountain" (11:23) (the Mount of Olives, we infer from the context), also is a reminiscence of a saying of Jesus about prayer

14. Josephus, *Antiquities*, 20:8, sec. 6.

for the coming of the Kingdom of God.[15] This, of course, was the central concern in the "Lord's Prayer." When the Kingdom comes, according to this prophetic tradition, *this* mountain indeed would be moved! Then, also, Mt. Zion would be raised (Isa. 2:2).

Later, on the Mount of Olives, Mark reports, four of Jesus' disciples asked him when the final events will occur (Mark 13:3 f.), and he answered them with the "synoptic apocalypse" (13: 5–37). After they ate the "Last Supper" together—in which Jesus spoke and acted in terms of the imminent coming of the Kingdom of God—Jesus and his disciples went back to the Mount of Olives (Mark 14:26). Were they hoping that God or His Kingdom might now appear there? Gathered on the Mount of Olives, the disciples again asked Jesus (now resurrected) whether he now "will restore the Kingdom of Israel" (Acts 1:6–12). The ascension took place here, and here two angels announce to the gaping disciples that Jesus would return in the same fashion, presumably to the same place. However else one may interpret the Acts story, it, together with the synoptic tradition, indicates a special eschatological significance for the Mount of Olives.

The ass's colt.—The Markan account of Jesus' entry into Jerusalem very likely is informed by the prophecies of the Messiah's entry contained in Gen. 49:11 and Zech. 9:9. In both places, an ass's colt is specified.[16] Rabbinic sources regard both the passages and the ass as messianic.[17] The description of the colt as "tied" seems to draw upon the reference in Genesis, while the stipulation that no one should have sat on it previously also implies royal or messianic import. Should the King of Israel sit on a beast that had previously borne secular riders? (Cf. Esther 6:8.) The outcry of Jesus' companions assumes their recognition of the eschatological, if not messianic, character of the scene. The later evangelists interpret it as such, including Luke, who for apologetic purposes

15. Thus also William Manson, *Jesus the Messiah* (Philadelphia: Westminster Press, 1946), p. 65. The Mount of Olives and the fig tree were on the way between Bethany and Jerusalem, and it is in this vicinity that Mark locates the episode. Mark 11:24 no longer presupposes a specific and eschatological setting; as it stands, it represents a later generalization in the direction of magic, psychologizing, and fideism (cf. I Cor. 13:2b).

16. See Heinz-Wolfgang Kuhn, "Das Reittier Jesu in der Einzugsgeschichte des Markusevangeliums," *ZNW* 50 (1959):82–91.

17. Ibid., pp. 87–89.

might have been expected to suppress or revise the political over-tones.

The decisive question here is whether the scene was so intended and understood by Jesus, or whether it owes its messianic character to the church's later reinterpretation on the basis of Old Testament prophecies. It is certainly possible that the latter is the case. Even if Jesus did ride into Jerusalem on an ass or the foal of an ass, it does not necessarily follow that he understood this mode of travel to have any special significance. On the other hand, there is no reason to suppose that Jesus himself was not familiar with these traditions or that he could or would not have applied them to him-self and acted accordingly. The tradition reports no other oc-casions when Jesus rode an ass or colt. He had instructed his dis-ciples to find him one for this occasion, and they had done so.

It was not an animal which he had ridden from Galilee, but one chosen for the specific (and short) journey from the Mount of Olives into Jerusalem. So far as we know, he did not use it again on his trips back and forth between Jerusalem and Bethany. Un-less Mark invented the description of the disciples' behavior (11:7), it would appear that they had some reason to consider this to be more than an ordinary animal, rider, and occasion. According to Luke 19:11, they "supposed that the Kingdom of God was to appear immediately"—with good reason! Luke knew, of course, that the Kingdom of God had not then come. He suggests that Jesus did not share this disappointed hope, and thus was not him-self mistaken, but undertook to explain the prospective delay by telling them the "parable of the pounds."[18] It is obvious, however, that this parable was not originally told in this context. It has a different purpose; moreover, the behavior of Jesus' disciples and other followers immediately afterward shows that they had not been deterred from this hope. Rather, as Luke tells us, it seems that they were looking for the imminent appearance of the Kingdom.

What was Jesus doing, riding an ass's colt from the Mount of Olives to Jerusalem, a distance of scarcely a mile? It seems likely that he was doing so intentionally to fulfill the prophetic descrip-tion of Zech. 9:9, in expectation that the Kingdom of God was soon to be established there and over all the earth (Zech. 9:10; 14:4-

18. Cf. Luke 24:21a, Acts 1:6 f., and Luke's omission of the saying at Mark 13:32.

11).[19] What else would he have expected his followers to conclude from this procession?

Garments, branches, and the ovation of "the many."—Mark does not say who "the many" were who spread their garments and "leafy branches" on the road, shouting "Hosanna!" as Jesus rode upon the ass's foal from the Mount of Olives to Jerusalem. Were they disciples or part of the larger group that had been following Jesus from Galilee and Jericho? Matthew interprets it to mean the latter (21:8 f.). Luke, who omits mention of branches, attributes the outcry to "the disciples" (19:37, 39). At all events, their procedure indicates recognition of Jesus either as Messiah or as "the Coming One," the prophetic forerunner for the Messianic Age.

Spreading garments before the procession of a monarch is evidently a gesture of deference or humility, symbolizing perhaps prostration, and in effect preparing a "royal carpet" for the exalted one to pass over. One can only speculate as to the origin of the practice of cutting and spreading branches. Conceivably it signified royalty, specifically, the hoped-for Messiah who should come forth like a "branch" from the stump of Davidic lineage (Isa. 11:1). "Branch" had become a standard term for the expected messiah(s).[20] At any rate, branches had been used by Jews to celebrate deliverance from their enemies since the second century BC (Judith 15:12 f.; I Macc. 13:51; II Macc. 10:7). In the last instance the cleansing of the Temple by Judas was also part of the occasion for rejoicing. Jesus, too, was about to cleanse the Temple. As yet, there had been no victory or deliverance. Those who scattered garments and branches along the way seem to have been celebrating a deliverance which was about to take place.

Such, precisely, is the substance of their ovation. If the "Hosanna" of Psalm 118 was repeated here, it may well have expressed hope that the salvation besought (118:25 f.) was coming, somehow, in connection with Jesus' entry. Such an exclamation had been addressed to the King in ancient Israel as a call for help (II Sam. 14:4; II Kings 6:26). Those shouting "Hosanna" were not simply repeating a hymn in observance of one of the annual festivals. If their spreading garments and branches does not make clear

19. Thus also Evans, "I Will Go Before," p. 5; Robert M. Grant, "The Coming of the Kingdom," *JBL* 67 (1948):297 ff. See also Isa. 62, esp. v. 11.
20. Jer. 23:5; Zech. 3:8; 4:12–14; 6:12.

the eschatological character of the occasion, their shouts of blessing upon "the Coming One" and the coming Kingdom should do so.[21] The outcry was occasioned by the advent of Jesus. The Aramaic- or Hebrew-speaking multitude would not have needed to be told that Jesus' name Yēshūa‘, Joshua, implied "salvation" (cf. Isa. 62:11b, "Behold, your salvation [Yēsha‘] comes"). The same root (yasha‘) appears in their exclamation "Hosanna." Those who knew the prophecy of Zech. 9:9 (whether or not they were cognizant of the earlier passage, 6:11, where a certain Joshua is named as the one who will be the Messiah) might well have believed that this Joshua who was mounted on the ass's foal was indeed the "Coming One," if not the King, the precursor of the time of Salvation. An earlier Joshua had led his people into the Land of Promise (Deut. 34:9; Josh. 1:1 ff.). To be sure, the cry "Blessed be he who comes in the name of the Lord!" may be derived from Psalm 118:26a, where it is not messianic but refers to the traveler entering the city to take part in the observances. But as the ovation is reported here, it refers to the Coming One, possibly Elijah, or (as Matthew and Luke interpret it) the Messiah, i.e., King or "Son of David."

In either case, the coming of the Messianic Age is in view. Elijah was to be its herald. The appearance of the Messiah could only mean its virtual imminence. Conceivably the outcry expresses the understanding that the Kingdom of the Messiah would precede the establishment of the Kingdom of God (cf. I Cor. 15:23 f.). But the idea of a preliminary "Kingdom" of the Messiah or Son of man appears only in the special Matthean and Lukan material in the synoptic Gospels. In general, the synoptic tradition expects the Messiah (or Son of man) to have a prominent place in the Kingdom of God: as Judge. The Kingdom of God would bring the Messiah, or the two would appear simultaneously.

It has often been asserted that Jesus opposed the "crude" or "political" messianic ideas of his contemporaries, and tried to teach instead a spiritual conception of the Messiah or Kingdom of God. Those who hold this view generally have final recourse to Luke 17:20 f., but that text probably refers to the future, visible, and un-

---

21. Thus also Eric Werner, " 'Hosanna' in the Gospels," *JBL* 65 (1946): 97–122; Kenneth J. Spencer, Jr., " 'Hosanna' and the Purpose of Jesus," *JBL* 67 (1948):171–76; J. Blenkinsopp "The Oracle of Judah and the Messianic Entry," *JBL* 80 (1961):55–64.

mistakable arrival of the Kingdom of God.[22] Jesus did not attempt
to quench the zeal of those who saw in his coming the sign that
the Kingdom was near. According to "Q" tradition, Jesus endorses
the outcry of his companions: " 'Hosanna to the Son of David' "
is "perfect praise" (Matt. 21:15 f.). If his followers had kept silent
—as "the Pharisees" thought they should—"the very stones would
cry out" (Luke 19:40). In effect, as in the Bartimaeus episode,
Jesus rebuked those who rebuked those who hailed him as Messiah.
It does not follow that Jesus either regarded himself or was regarded by his followers as a military-political revolutionary (cf.
John 6:15). Such interpretations do not take into account the
eschatological character of Jesus' beliefs: when the Kingdom of
God comes, God will bring it. God, not the Messiah, will overcome
the enemies of the Jews (Zech. 9:9 f.; 14:1-19). But the political
character of this expectation should not be ignored. When the
dominion of God is established over all the earth, the rule of the
Herods and the Romans, the quasi-Satanic principalities and
powers, will be finished. The Roman authorities, together with

22. See *KGST*, pp. 22–29. Those referred to as "they" in Luke 17:21 evidently are those who will witness the coming of the Kingdom at some point
in the future. Why, at that time, will they not say, "Lo, here it is!" or
"There!"? It makes no sense to urge that they will not then say so because
Jesus at some previous time had already manifested the Kingdom in the midst
of some Pharisees (much less, that it had been present "in their hearts").
Rather, they—the future witnesses of the coming of the Kingdom—will not
say "Lo, here (etc.)!" for the reason that when they see the Kingdom coming,
there will be no possible doubt about it. Such is clearly the meaning of Luke
17:23 f. with respect to the appearance of the Son of man, in effect: "All
flesh will see it together." Thus also Pannenberg, *Jesus—God and Man*, pp.
226–27; cf. Enslin, *Prophet*, p. 71: "The Age to Come, the new age, will
suddenly and spectacularly appear." See also Luke 21:34–36.

That Jesus' understanding of the Kingdom of God was "purely spiritual" is extremely doubtful. Synoptic sources report that he expected that, in
the new era, both he and his disciples would be sitting on thrones and eating
and drinking at table with the patriarchs. H. S. Reimarus, who was one of the
first to appreciate the wholly futuristic character of Jesus' expectations concerning the Kingdom, was alert to the fact that Jesus was talking about the
establishment of God's kingdom on earth, a "secular" kingdom. Roman authorities would no longer rule; the Messiah or God would rule the earth in
those days. What Reimarus did not notice was that Jesus expected *God* to
bring the Kingdom. After two hundred years, Reimarus' principal study on this
subject has become available to English readers under two different titles
and in two different translations, both appearing the same year, 1970: *Fragments* (Philadelphia: Fortress Press), and *The Goal of Jesus and His Disciples*
(Leiden: Brill). See, for instance, the latter, esp. pp. 85–125.

those Jews who looked to Rome in hope or fear as their ultimate earthly sovereign, were not acting without reference to the political scene when they concerted to do away with the one whose proclamation, and now whose presence in Jerusalem, aroused some number of Jews to enthusiasm for the coming of the Kingdom of God.

19. THE PRAYER ABOUT NOT EATING FIGS (MARK 11:12–14)

Only a few hours after his "triumphal" entry as the "Coming One" or Messiah, Jesus again went to Jerusalem from Bethany, this time evidently on foot. Being hungry, Mark says, Jesus stopped by a flourishing fig tree, only to find no figs. Despite the fact that it was "not the season for figs," Jesus seems to have been exasperated, and apparently commanded that no one eat again of its fruit *eis ton aiōna* ("ever")—a strange performance for one who had cautioned his own followers not to be anxious about food but to seek first the Kingdom of God (Matt. 6:25–34)!

In order to make Jesus' action more coherent, it has been suggested that the fig tree episode occurred at Tabernacles rather than Passover: in that case, it would have been the season for figs after all.[23] This is not impossible, though it would then be necessary to explain why Mark changed the setting, thereby creating the seeming irrationality of Jesus' expectation. It would also still need to be explained why Jesus swore (or prayed?) that no one should eat its figs again *eis ton aiōna*.

Aside from its context—between the eschatological if not also messianic entrance and the eschatological if not messianic cleansing of the Temple—a number of considerations point to the conclusion that Jesus' reaction to the fig tree was prompted by his own eschatological-messianic beliefs.

There is ample evidence in prophetic, intertestamental, New Testament, early Christian, and rabbinical literature to the effect that in the Messianic Age the primordial curse upon the ground would be removed, and nature would bring forth its fruit in perennial and preternatural abundance (e.g., Isa. 32:15; *Syr.*

23. Charles W. F. Smith, "No Time for Figs," *JBL* 79 (1960):315–27.

Baruch 29:5–8).[24] The expectation is part of the whole vision of a transformed world in which nature will no longer be harsh, or food and water—thus also health and life—marginal and insecure (cf. Zech. 14:6–8). The imagery and expectation of the inaugural, if not perpetual, Messianic Banquet also gives expression to this hope (e.g., Isa. 25:6).

It would have been strange if Jesus was hungry, for he had just come from his camp at Bethany, less than an hour's distance.[25] Furthermore, they were now nearly to Jerusalem. Could he not find something else to eat? Why did he not dispatch one of his disciples for food? Was the problem that he was hungry, or that the fig tree failed him in some other way? Was he looking for the beginning "this day" of the superabundance of nature that was to mark the arrival of the Messianic Age? In the Messianic Age, fruit would always be in season!

It is not certain, however, that Jesus was disappointed in not finding figs, although his words may have appeared in such a light to his companions at the time. Mark's version of Jesus' saying does not necessarily take the form of a "curse," though Mark himself— how much more Matthew!—seems to have so construed it in the legendary sequel (Mark 11:20 f.).[26] By itself the saying seems rather to have been a vow or prayer.

In the world view of Judaism at the time, there were two ages or eras, the Present age and the Coming age. The statement or idea behind the expression *eis ton aiōna* could not have meant simply "ever."[27] It probably would have meant, literally, "in the

24. E.g., also Ezek. 17:22 ff.; Joel 3:18; Rev. 22:1 f. See my article "Not the Season for Figs."

25. So also Hans-Werner Bartsch, "Die 'Verfluchung' des Feigenbaums," *ZNW* 53 (1962):257. Bethany is about two miles from Jerusalem.

26. Reference to "cursing" appears only in the sequel. Matthew changes Jesus' words from an oath or prayer about not eating figs to a curse, "May you produce no more figs" (Matt. 21:19b), and has the tree wither instantly as if scorched by a flame-thrower. The episode is commonly read by Christian interpreters in an anti-Jewish sense, e.g., Schweizer, *Jesus*, p. 8: "For Mark, this barren fig tree is the symbol of an exclusivist Judaism that will not open itself to the nations of the world, and whose time is past." This is possible, of course, though Mark (who probably had not read the Fourth Gospel) does not report any other blanket condemnations of Judaism by Jesus. And even if such were Mark's understanding, there is no reason to suppose that it had also been Jesus'.

27. So also Bartsch, " 'Verfluchung,' " p. 258.

(Present) age" or, more likely, "until the (Coming) age" (*le 'olam,* '*ad-'olme-'ad*). In either case the sense would be, "May no one eat your fruit again until the Kingdom of God comes."

Jesus uttered a similar oath or prayer somewhat later, this time with reference to the observance of Passover, or perhaps the weekly or daily act of drinking wine: "I shall not drink again of the fruit of the vine until that day when I drink it new in the Kingdom of God" (Mark 14:25; cf. Luke 22:16, 18).

Jesus was now about to enter Jerusalem, apparently for the second time. The Kingdom had not yet come, despite his earlier expectations and despite his entrance the previous day in fulfillment of Zech. 9:9. But he still hopes that it will do so in the near future. As he is about to venture upon his dangerous mission in Jerusalem, the purification of the Temple, he passes a fig tree, perhaps in bud or bloom (cf. Mark 13:28). Jesus' own prayers and his instructions to his followers about prayer—like the rest of his teaching, preaching, and activity—were focused upon the coming of the Kingdom of God. Now, at this critical moment, he prays— not a public prayer, but still "his disciples heard it": "May no one eat your fruit again until the Age to Come." As in the case of the saying about the "fruit of the vine," Jesus may have been referring to fig trees generally, the fruit of any fig tree. Or he may have had in mind this particular tree located near the Mount of Olives and Jerusalem. In any case, the prayer was addressed to God: that He would bring His Kingdom soon. If it was somewhat before Passover, figs would be ripe in about eight weeks.[28]

If such was Jesus' prayer, it was not answered. The season for figs came, but the Kingdom of God did not. Perhaps not even the disciples who overheard the prayer had understood what he meant. Later, tradition turned the prayer into a miracle story: the saying had its "fulfillment" in the reported fate of the fig tree (11:20 f.). If the tree died, naturally no one would eat again of its fruit! As in the case of the meal(s) in the wilderness and the exorcism traditions, what was once a matter of eschatological importance has been generalized into a miracle story.

28. Ibid. The vine and the fig tree often, together, represent the ideal life in the Promised land and Messianic age: e.g., I Kings 4:25; Mic. 4:4; Zech. 3:10.

20. THE PURIFICATION OF THE TEMPLE (MARK 11:15–17)

On the same day as his entry into Jerusalem, according to Matthew
and Luke, or the next day in Mark's version, Jesus entered the
Temple, forcibly terminating the activities of buyers and sellers (of
sacrificial animals?) and money-changers, and stopping those who
wished to carry anything through the Temple.

It would be possible to explain this behavior partly as the reaction of an outraged rural reformer against the profit-seeking inno-
vations of the business-priestly establishment.[29] The Fourth Gospel
treats it as fulfilling the "prophecy" of Ps. 69:9, a text which his
disciples "remembered" afterward even though it had no eschatological import (John 2:17). But the words which John attributes
to Jesus (2:16) clearly echo the eschatological pronouncement of
Zech. 14:21b: "And there shall no longer be a trader in the house
of the Lord of hosts on that day."

Whether John (or an earlier commentator) supplied the allusion
or whether it goes back to a saying of Jesus, the Zechariah passage
seems to have been, at least in part, the basis for Jesus' action. It
may be, also, that Jesus' prohibition against carrying things through
the Temple was based upon a reading of Zech. 14:21a, to the effect
that only sacred vessels should be used in the Temple in the
Messianic Age. At any rate, Jesus' action in ejecting the buyers and
sellers, and possibly also the money-changers, seems to be based
on his assumption that he was acting to prepare the Temple for
the inauguration of "that day," the Messianic Age, in accordance
with Zech. 14:20 f.[30] Earlier, he had entered Jerusalem in accordance with the prophecy of Zech. 9:9. Moreover, Jesus' name, Joshua
(*Yehōshūaʿ* or *Yēshūaʿ*), was the same as that of the priestly messiah
whose task it would be to "rule my house and have charge of my
courts" (Zech. 3:6) and, ultimately, to complete the Temple (Zech.

29. For variations on this thesis, see Victor Eppstein, "The Historicity of
the Gospel Account of the Cleansing of the Temple," ZNW 55 (1964):42–
58; Hugh J. Schonfield, *The Passover Plot* (New York: Bernard Geis Associates, 1966), p. 123; and Étienne Trocmé, "L'expulsion des marchands du
Temple," NTS 15 (1968):1–22. In common, these interpreters proceed without reference to Jesus' hope for the coming of the Kingdom of God. But cf.
Morton S. Enslin, "The Temple and the Cross," *Judaism* 20 (1971):24–31.

30. So also Cecil Roth, "The Cleansing of the Temple and Zechariah,"
NT 4 (1960):174–81; Neill Q. Hamilton, "Temple Cleansing and Temple
Bank," JBL 83 (1964):365–72.

6:11–15; cf. II Sam. 7:12–16). The expectation that a priestly messiah would restore Israel and the Temple at the end of the age also appears in the Qumran literature.[31]

Temple reforms had traditionally been associated with efforts to inaugurate political independence, both in Israel and elsewhere in the Near East.[32] The Romans and their Jewish collaborators may well have interpreted Jesus' action in the Temple as equivalent to a kingly claim.[33] Jesus was subsequently charged and executed as a pretender to the Jewish kingship.

Another Old Testament text may have been in Jesus' mind also, Mal. 3:1–3. Here, as in the case of the ovation on the way to the city, there is a curious ambiguity as to the precise title and role. Is "he" in Mal. 3:2–3 God's "messenger" of the covenant who "is coming" (3:1) or "the Lord" who "will suddenly come to his [God's?] Temple?" Or are the coming "Messenger" and the coming "Lord" (hā'ādōn, not YHWH) the same, in apposition, after the pattern of repetition or parallelism characteristic of Hebrew poetry? If Jesus understood himself to be fulfilling this prophecy, was it as "messenger," "Coming One," or Messiah? We cannot tell. But his activity in effect is to "purify the sons of Levi," i.e., to cause the Temple procedures to be made right (3:3).[34] In Malachi, the Temple purification was regarded as the one thing needed to clear the way for God to "pour down . . . an overflowing blessing" (3:10); afterward, judgment and redemption would take place (3:4 f., 11 f.). Whether Jesus would have connected the coming messenger of Mal. 3:1 with the coming Elijah of Mal. 4:5 cannot be determined.[35] If so, his action in the Temple would have been that of the eschatological Elijah, a role which he then would have shared with John the Baptist.[36] Whether as "Messenger," Elijah, "Coming One," or Messiah (or some combination of these roles), Jesus' ac-

31. IQH 2:20 ff. Also T. Levi 18. See Betz, "Heiliger Krieg," pp. 134–35.
32. E.g., II Kings 18:4–7; 22:3—23:30. See Spencer, " 'Hosanna,' " p. 172.
33. Thus Hamilton, "Temple Cleansing," pp. 370–71, and Betz, What Do We Know?, p. 91.
34. So also J. W. Doeve, "Purification de Temple et Deséchement du Figuier," NTS 1 (1954–55):305–6.
35. But it is likely that he did. See Matt. 11:9 f., 14, and Hiers, "Purification of the Temple: Preparation for the Kingdom of God," JBL 90 (1971):82–90, esp. p. 88n24.
36. Thus also Spencer, " 'Hosanna,' " p. 172. See Robinson, "Elijah, John, and Jesus," pp. 28 ff., for other suggestions in this connection.

88   THE HISTORICAL JESUS AND THE KINGDOM OF GOD

tion in the Temple was eschatological: by purifying it, he was making ready for "that day," the coming of the Kingdom of God.[37]

The same seems to be indicated in his reported saying that the Temple "shall be called a house of prayer for all the nations" (Mark 11:17a). The future tense reflects the fact that the oracle cited (Isa. 56:7) was understood to refer to the future Messianic Age, the time of "salvation" and deliverance (Isa. 56:1; cf. 65:17–25). The idea that in the Messianic Age all nations (the "Gentiles") will worship God in the Jerusalem Temple is a persistent theme in Jewish eschatological literature.[38] In that age, the alienation characteristic of human affairs since the beginning of historical existence (Gen. 3–11) would be overcome. Nations would live at peace with one another, and productivity of nature and harmony between man and all other living beings would be restored.[39] If Jesus declared that Gentiles were now to worship in the Temple, it could have been only because the advent of the Messianic Age was at hand. Understandably, "all the multitude was astonished at his teaching" (Mark 11:18)![40] It is quite possible, however, that this saying about "all the nations" was added later in the development of the tradition, to justify the inclusion of Gentiles in the Church (cf. Mark 13:10). But it seems less likely that the Church would have invented the story of Jesus' actions in the Temple, actions which seem to reflect the Zechariah and Malachi texts which were not otherwise appropriated by the Church.

Perhaps Jesus kept returning to the Temple for several days in order to enforce his attempted reformation of the cultus. Mark indicates that at least two days were spent there, and that it was on the second day that the Temple authorities questioned his authority "for doing these things" (11:27 f.). Luke gives the impression that Jesus spent many days in the Temple, mainly teaching or preaching (19:47; 20:1; 21:37 f.). Jesus' response to the ques-

37. So also Rudolf Bultmann, *Jesus and the Word* (New York: Scribner, 1958), p. 29; and Grässer, *Parusieverzögerung*, pp. 27–28.
38. See esp. Isa. 2:2–4 (Mic. 4:1–4); Isa. 25:7; 66:18–23; Zech. 14:16–19; *T. Levi* 18:9; Rev. 21:23–26; cf. Isa. 19:19–24; 49:6.
39. See Gerhard von Rad, *Genesis* (Philadelphia: Westminster, 1961), pp. 149–50, 155–56. E.g., Isa. 11:6–9. Cf. *Syr. Baruch* 73–74.
40. This idea may have been the basis for the later mission to the Gentiles. The Church, in time, seems to have become convinced that the Kingdom could come only after the Gospel had been preached to "all nations" (Matt. 28:19 f.; Mark 13:10 = Matt. 24:14; cf. Luke 21:24b; Rom. 11:25 f.). How could the Gentiles worship God if they had not heard the Gospel?

tion about his authority links his work with that of the Baptist (Mark 11:29–33). Together they shared the work of preparation for the coming of the Kingdom. In John, Elijah had come. Now in the person of Jesus, the Coming one—or the Messiah (?)—had come to the Temple, as it was "written" that he should (Mal. 3:1—4:6).

Jesus was doing what he believed on the basis of Scripture to be his divinely appointed mission. He had come to Jerusalem to prepare that city and the Temple for the coming of the Kingdom. It now remained for the Kingdom to come. It also remained to be seen how long the authorities would tolerate his presence in the Temple. Since they did not share his belief that God's Kingdom was about to be established, they had to think not only of the need to defend their own prerogatives, but also of their responsibility for maintaining order and for avoiding Roman intervention. Something would have to be done.

21. "NOT FAR FROM THE KINGDOM OF GOD" (MARK 12:34)

We do not know how many days Jesus kept returning to the Temple obstructing the buyers, sellers, and money-changers and teaching the multitudes. Nor do we know precisely the substance of his teaching. Some of it seems to have been in response to various challenges on the part of the religious hierarchy, who were hoping to embarrass him before the crowds and/or find grounds for having him arrested and disposed of by the Romans (e.g., Mark 11:27–33; 12:13–27; and possibly 12:35–37a).

Generally, however, the teaching and parables attributed to Jesus during these days had to do with the kind of life that would be pleasing to God and appropriate in view of the prospective time of Judgment and Salvation. Some of it probably was reshaped or created by the early Church in accordance with its christological beliefs and the problem of the delay of the parousia.

The parable of the wicked tenants (Mark 12:1–12) may reflect such interests, though coming as it does immediately after Jesus' reference to the work of the Baptist, it is not impossible that its origin was in a saying or parable about John (cf. Matt. 23:37 = Luke 13:34). Whether or not it implies Jesus' awareness of his own impending fate, it does look to the transfer of the vineyard or Kingdom of God (Matt. 21:43) to other tenants. One must respond to the invitation before it is withdrawn (Matt. 22:1–10 = Luke 14:16–24). Only those who do the will of God may hope to enter his Kingdom (Matt. 21:28–32; Mark 12:38–40). Perhaps the several parables about "watching," being ready at all times, that were attached by Matthew and Luke to the synoptic apocalypse also were spoken in the Temple or, at any rate, in its vicinity and not long after the Temple sayings (e.g., Matt. 24:37—25:30 and parallels).

While Jesus was teaching in the Temple, a scribe asked him which was the most important commandment (Mark 12:28–34). It was not an uncommon type of question for a Jew to ask of a rabbi. In effect, it was like that asked by the rich "young" man at the outset of Jesus' journey to Jerusalem (Mark 10:17 ff.), though the scribe does not ask specifically what he must do to enter the Kingdom. In both cases, Jesus responded by referring to the Law: in the earlier instance to the "second table" of the Decalogue, in the latter to Deut. 6:5 and Lev. 19:18. In each case, the questioner affirmed what Jesus said. In the earlier instance, Jesus added the further instruction "follow me"—to Jerusalem. There was no such additional instruction here. They were already in Jerusalem. Instead, Jesus answered, "You are not far from the Kingdom of God."

Jesus did not qualify his assurance to the scribe by saying that he was almost fit for admission into the Kingdom, as if there were still something else he must do first, or as if he had just barely failed his final examination. Instead, Mark interpreted Jesus' statement as a commendation, in view of the fact that the scribe had "answered wisely." No fault is to be found with his answer. He had said, "You are right, teacher; you have truly said that he is one, and there is no other but he; and to love him with all the heart and with all the understanding, and with all the strength, and to love one's neighbor as oneself, is much more than all whole burnt offerings and sacrifices." Such an answer shows him to be one who is worthy to enter. He is not far from the Kingdom of God: it will not be long until the Kingdom of God comes. He has only to wait.[41] This assurance has

41. The saying may also include an intimation that the Kingdom is spatially near. That the Kingdom of God exists in heaven is assumed. Jesus and his followers pray and look for its coming to earth. The temporal nearness of the

its negative counterpart in the "Q" saying which Matthew includes later in this context: the blood of all the prophets of antiquity will be required of the unrighteous of *this* generation (Matt. 23:34–36= Luke 11:49–51). Judgment and Salvation are at hand.

22. THE DESTRUCTION OF THE TEMPLE (MARK 13:1–2)

The saying attributed to Jesus at Mark 13:2 may simply be an instance of *vaticinium ex eventu*, prophecy after the fact.[42] If Mark wrote after 70 AD, he would have recognized that the Kingdom had not come with the Jewish war of 66–70 and the consequent destruction of the Temple. Mark 13:8 intimates that warfare of nation against nation is only the beginning of the *ōdin*, birth pangs of the Messianic Age. Its arrival is to come (13:26 f.) only after several other signs and happenings (13:9, 10, 14–20, 21 ff., 24 f.) have taken place. On the other hand, the fact that the Temple was not destroyed completely, as predicted in 13:2, suggests that the evangelist may have written before 70 AD. Quite a few stones of Herod's Temple remain in their original place atop one another to the present time.[43] The warfare described in Mark 13:8 could be simply part of the traditional apocalyptic imagery (e.g., Zech. 14:2) rather than an ex post facto reference to the Jewish-Roman war. It may be, then, that Jesus did prophesy the destruction of the Temple as part of the eschatological fulfillment. Various New Testament traditions seem to represent efforts to explain away such a saying (e.g., the "false" accusations reported in Mark 14:58; 15:29; Acts 6:13 f.; cf. John 2:19 f.).[44]

The destruction of the Temple is prophesied in conjunction with the coming of the Messianic Age in Mic. 3:12, and later in Jer.

Kingdom is correlated to its spatial nearness. Thus J. Weiss; see also Enslin, *Prophet*, p. 72: "At the moment it was present only as are the clouds in heaven which cast upon the earth their shadow." Cf. Cranfield, *St. Mark*, pp. 67–68, 380; he urges that the Kingdom was present in Jesus, "the *autobasileia*," from whom the scribe was spatially "not far."

42. So argues Nikolaus Walter, "Tempelzerstörung und synoptische Apokalypse," *ZNW* 57 (1966):38–49.

43. William F. Stinespring, "Wilson's Arch Revisited," *BA* 29 (1966):27–36, and "Wilson's Arch and the Masonic Hall," *BA* 30 (1967):27–31.

44. So also Aune, "Messianic Secret," pp. 24–25. Aune proposes, implausibly, that the Temple Jesus meant to build was the Church.

7:11 ff., as part of God's judgment in the coming days. According to Mark 11:17b, Jesus quotes, or alludes to, Jer. 7:11 in berating the Temple officialdom. One might conjecture that, after a few days, Jesus saw that the members of the priestly hierarchy had not changed their ways, that they had not accepted the purification he had attempted to bring as God's messenger. Even if he did not know that they were plotting against him, he could sense their hostility. Therefore, the destruction foretold in the rest of the prophecy would come to pass: Zion would become like Shiloh (Jer. 7:12–14).[45] It was precisely as he ceased holding forth in the Temple that Jesus made his statement about the Temple's destruction. He had done what he could here. He did not set foot in it again.

It is not certain that Jesus' Jewish contemporaries looked for the destruction of the Temple at the advent of the Messianic Age. There is a reference to it in Tobit 14:4 ff. (c. 150 BC), but this probably refers retrospectively to the events of 587–86. Of course, this, like the passages in Micah and Jeremiah, could have been construed literalistically as prophecy for the era of the reader. It may be significant that Mark joins the question when "this" expectation will be fulfilled to the question when "all these things" (the eschatological phenomena described in the verses following) are to be accomplished (13:4). Evidently Mark, if not also Jesus' disciples, understood the destruction of the Temple as an eschatological event, one which Jesus himself had foretold, even if the charge that he himself would destroy it was false. The fact that Luke subsequently "historicized" the destruction of the Temple[46] is further confirmation of its original eschatological significance.

Conceivably, the tradition that the veil of the Temple curtain was torn in two as Jesus expired (Mark 15:38) expresses the idea that, with his death, the Messianic Age should have begun: the Temple was destroyed, at least symbolically (cf. Isa. 25:7). The

45. Cf. Gen. 49:10b, "until Shiloh comes." Jesus had entered as the Judahite Messiah. Now should not Shiloh—the destruction of the Temple— come to pass? See also Jer. 26:18 = Mic. 3:12. Note that Micah's famous prophecy about the Messianic Age (4:1–4) follows immediately after his declaration that "Zion shall be plowed as a field." After the destruction of the Temple comes the Messianic Age.

46. See William C. Robinson, Jr., Der Weg Des Herrn, Theologische Forschung 36 (Hamburg-Bergstedt: Herbert Reich, 1964), pp. 46 ff. Cf. Fred O. Francis, "Eschatology and History in Luke–Acts," JAAR 37 (1969):55–58.

other phenomena reported in the Gospels at this point are clearly eschatological in character, and none of them is reported outside of Christian literature (Mark 15:33 and parallels; Matt. 27:51b–53).[47] Perhaps Mark understood that with the tearing of the Temple curtain the prophecy of 13:2 was symbolically fulfilled. There is no reference to any further destruction of the Temple in the apocalyptic program set forth in Mark 13:5–37, contrary to what one might expect from 13:1 f.

Weiss suggests that Jesus anticipated the destruction of the Temple in connection with the general break-up of the Old world which would occur at the end of the Present age.[48] "All these things" would take place soon, during the lifetime of Jesus' contemporaries (Mark 13:30). Heaven and earth would pass away (13:31; cf. Isa. 65:17; 66:22). Would not the Temple "pass away" as well? Rabbi Eliezer (c. 90 AD) thought that the Messianic Age should have begun when the Temple was destroyed by Titus.[49] It is probable that Jesus—after the failure of his attempt to purify the Temple, if not even before—expected that with the coming of the Kingdom of God the old Temple would be destroyed. Once the Messiah has come and creation redeemed, what need would there be for priests and sacrifices?[50]

But it is not impossible that Jesus also had spoken of a new Temple which he would build: this may be the germ of truth in the charge brought against him by his accusers (Mark 14:58 and parallels). The priestly Messiah of Zechariah (whose name, too, was Joshua) had as his chief assignment the task of rebuilding the Temple, in effect, building a new Temple (Zech. 6:11–13). If Jesus was to fulfill this task, which had been assigned to one bearing his name, and build the Temple, the old Temple must first be destroyed. Once the new Temple was built, according to Zech. 1–8, the Era of blessing would begin. Likewise, the "Son of David" of II Sam. 7:13 was to build the new Temple, whereupon God

47. Thus also Werner, *The Formation of Christian Dogma*, p. 33. Note also Jesus' words to the thief (Luke 23:43). Did Jesus himself expect the Kingdom to come "today," the day of his execution?

48. *Predigt* (1900), p. 106.

49. Billerbeck, 1:163.

50. Cf. Jer. 7:22 f. The Old Testament prophets were generally opposed at any rate to the offering of sacrifices, in lieu of justice and mercy. In the vision of the new earth and new Jerusalem in Rev. 21, there would be no Temple (21:22).

would establish his Kingdom forever. Johannine tradition claims that Jesus had claimed that he would "raise up" the Temple, though here the Fourth Evangelist has demythologized or christologized the import of the saying (John 2:19–22). If Jesus claimed that he would build (or rebuild) the Temple, this would have been a messianic claim. It may have led to the accusation that he had claimed to be Messiah.[51]

Whether Jesus spoke of the destruction of the Temple or of the building of a new one, or both, the meaning of such a prospect could only have been eschatological. Later, in fact, the Temple of Herod would be, for the most part, destroyed. But the Kingdom of God would not yet come, in Jerusalem or anywhere else on earth.

23. THE ANOINTING AT BETHANY (MARK 14:3–9)

The title "messiah" means literally "one who is anointed," i.e., on whose head oil is poured, symbolizing his appointment by God as King (e.g., I Sam. 10:1; 16:1–13; II Kings 9:1–6). The presence of God's Spirit is generally assumed (cf. Isa. 11:2).

The story of Jesus' baptism by John may have been written with the understanding that Jesus was anointed on this occasion, though with water rather than oil. As he came out of the water, he saw the Spirit of God descending upon him (Mark 1:10 and parallels). The voice from heaven repeated the pronouncement from the ancient Israelite coronation liturgy: "You are my son, today I have begotten you" (Ps. 2:7). The words denote messiahship, not divinity. According to Justin Martyr, Jews of the second century expected Elijah to anoint the Messiah and bear witness to him as such. It is possible that Jesus' own "messianic self-consciousness" dates from his baptismal experience, particularly if he had already recognized the Baptist as Elijah. But it is not evident that John or anyone else recognized Jesus as the Messiah on this occasion (n.b.,

---

51. See Betz, *What Do We Know?*, pp. 88–91, and Bertil Gärtner, *The Temple and the Community in Qumran and the New Testament* (Cambridge: At the University Press, 1965), pp. 16–17, 105–6. The expectation of a new Temple in the Messianic Age appears at numerous places in the Jewish literature, e.g., Ezek. 37:26–28; 40—48; *Jubilees* 1:28 f.; *I Enoch* 90:28 f.; *Sibylline Oracles* 5:414–33. In these passages, and often elsewhere, God Himself is expected to bring or create the new Temple; there is no mention of a Messiah.

Matt. 11:2 f.), or that anyone but Jesus could as yet have recognized John as Elijah.

Luke, like the Fourth Evangelist, does not actually have John baptize Jesus, probably in order to avoid the implication that Jesus needed forgiveness of sins; he moves the story of Jesus' anointing by "a woman" from Bethany to Galilee (Luke 7:37–50). The emphasis is changed from the significance of the anointing to the generosity and hospitality of the woman and to the forgiveness of sins, a particular interest of Luke. Instead of anointing his head, she washes, kisses, and anoints his feet. Luke makes no reference to burial. He also omits entirely the embarrassing question of why the woman did not sell the expensive ointment and give to the poor, and to Luke's point of view, the seemingly callous remark of Jesus that "you always have the poor with you" (Mark 14:7).[52]

The Markan version of the anointing at Bethany also seems to have been reworked somewhat in accordance with Christian interests. The explanation that the woman was anointing Jesus' body beforehand for burial (14:8) intimates foreknowledge of Jesus' death and burial, not only by Jesus, which is possible, but by the anonymous woman, which is unlikely. The verse following, which assumes the preaching of the Gospel throughout "the whole world," is certainly secondary, since the world mission of the Church did not begin before 40 AD. Furthermore, the assurance that the episode would be retold "in memory of her" implies that she was dead when these words were first composed.

If the actual anointing was not for burial, what else could it have signified if not the anointing of the one who was to be King? The Johannine version, secondary as it is with respect to content, is placed appropriately just before Jesus' messianic entrance into Jerusalem (12:1–8). One might speculate that the woman acted at the behest of Jesus himself, as his followers had done when they secured the ass for his entrance to the city and soon were to do in locating a room for their Passover supper. Could it be that the Kingdom had not come because the Messiah had not been properly anointed? The prophet John–Elijah was dead. Who was there now to anoint him? At any rate, as the story is told, Jesus

52. In the Messianic Age, of course, the poor would be provided for abundantly (Luke 6:20 f.; 16:9, 22, 25). But Luke was especially concerned that, in the meantime, Christians should do all they could for the poor (12: 32 f.).

was now anointed. Whether anyone, including Jesus himself, understood that he was thereby anointed as Messiah, we cannot tell.

24. THE LAST SUPPER AND THE KINGDOM OF GOD

It was no ordinary Passover meal that Jesus ate with his disciples in Jerusalem.[53] He and his followers had traveled all over Galilee proclaiming the nearness of the Kingdom of God and making ready for its arrival. It had not come. They had entered Jerusalem a few days earlier, expecting the Kingdom to be established soon. Perhaps Jesus had looked for it to appear as he entered the city the first time, or, perhaps, when he had cleansed the Temple. It still had not come. When would it come?

Jesus may have been aware that the authorities were looking for him. He waited until it was dark to enter the city (Mark 14:17). The situation was dangerous, but this was no time to go back to Galilee. The Passover must be kept in Jerusalem (Deut. 16:5 f.).

The saying about the Kingdom of God at the Last Supper is subject to various interpretations. The reference to the Passover (lamb) in Luke 22:15 f. implies that Jesus himself abstained from the meal, vowing that he would not eat it until it was fulfilled in the Kingdom of God, i.e., until the transcendent deliverance of the Messianic Age took place. The Passover will have its fulfillment in the Messianic Banquet.[54] A variant attested by good manuscripts implies that he does eat this Passover with them, but vows not to eat it again until he can do so in the Kingdom of God. Perhaps the saying implies that he expects that the Kingdom will come by the time of the next Passover. Or it could mean that he expects the fulfillment of the Passover, i.e., the Kingdom of God, at any time; it need not wait until the next Passover season.

The saying about the fruit of the vine supports this latter interpretation. Jesus says that he will not drink wine "again" until he

53. That it was a Passover meal has been argued convincingly by Joachim Jeremias, *The Eucharistic Words of Jesus* (Oxford: Basil Blackwell, 1955). However, cf. W. O. E. Oesterly, *The Jewish Background of the Christian Liturgy* (Oxford: Clarendon, 1925), pp. 156–204.

54. So A. J. B. Higgins, *The Lord's Supper in the New Testament*, SBT no. 6 (London: SCM, 1952), p. 47.

drinks it with his companions in the Kingdom of God. The next time he drinks wine will be at the messianic feast. In the meantime, he will abstain from drinking wine.[55] The sense is parallel to that of his prayer or oath (or injunction) about not eating the fruit of the fig tree (Mark 11:14): may the Kingdom of God come soon! The season for figs would come in few weeks. But one might expect to drink wine again, a common beverage at any meal, as early as the next day, and at any rate on the next Sabbath (which, according to Jeremias, would have been the next day). Was the vow also parallel, then, to the petition he had taught his disciples, "Give us our bread for tomorrow today" (Matt. 6:11)? Here, he says in effect, "Give us the wine of the messianic table by tomorrow."

It is to be noticed that the vow about drinking wine does not imply or suggest that Jesus understood that he must die before the Kingdom of God could come. Later that evening, he could still hope and pray that the Kingdom might come without his having to take up the cup of tribulation (Mark 14:33–39). It is conceivable that Jesus hoped, as perhaps he had hoped when he "fed" the crowds in the wilderness, that through proleptic or symbolic enactment of the Messianic Banquet, God might be induced to cause His Kingdom to come. At any rate, like John's baptism, the supper would have served to mark or consecrate its recipients as those who would also have a share in the Messianic Banquet. They had shared his trials; they would also share his prerogatives in the Age to come (cf. Luke 22:28–30). Did he perhaps hope that the Kingdom would come while he was gathered at table with his followers, as perhaps he had hoped and prayed at the banquet in the wilderness? Does the vow of abstinence from wine express the same kind of disappointment possibly implicit in the prayer or injunction about not eating figs: since the Kingdom has not yet come, may it do so before . . . ? Or did he consider the meal with his disciples, like the messianic entry and the cleansing of the Temple, a preliminary action to be carried out in preparation for the coming of the Kingdom of God? Immediately afterward, they went to the Mount of Olives. Did they hope that now the Kingdom or Messiah might be manifested there? If so, the next day they could drink wine anew in the Kingdom of God.

55. So also Joachim Jeremias, "The Last Supper," *JTS* 50 (1949):9–10; *Eucharistic Words*, pp. 165 ff.; and Cranfield, *St. Mark*, pp. 427–28.

As the story of the Last Supper is told, however, it is clear that the evangelists understood that Jesus realized that first he must die. This appears both in the saying that the "Son of man goes as it is written of him" (Mark 14:21) and the "blood of the covenant" saying (14:24). The "Son of man" saying appears to be tacked onto the saying about the betrayer: the link *hoti* ("because") is artificial, and Matthew omits it. The "blood of the covenant" concept may be derived from Zech. 9:11. That Jesus had earlier found clues to his own self-understanding and activity in Zechariah is probable. The early Church, to some extent, also utilized the book of Zechariah in writing its account of the passion narrative (e.g., Zech. 11:12 f.; 12:10). In many instances, it is impossible to determine whether a passage was first applied to Jesus by himself or by Christian tradition.

There are some other texts in Zechariah which could have influenced Jesus' thinking at this point. In Zech. 3:8–10, Joshua is told that God is about to "remove the guilt of this land in a single day," after which the Messiah ("Branch") and the Messianic Age will come. In Zech. 6, it is declared that Joshua (Jesus) himself is this Messiah! After the supper, according to Mark, Jesus cited Zech. 13:7 to explain the imminent "scattering" of his followers. In Zech. 3:8, the Messiah is referred to as "my servant," i.e., God's servant. The redemptive significance of the torment inflicted upon "my servant" is indicated in Isa. 52:13—53:12, but without any evident eschatological sense. II Sam. 7:12–16 refers to the possible chastening of the son of David, whose Kingdom shall be established forever, but the chastening is not given any redemptive meaning. In II Sam. 7:19–29, David speaks of himself repeatedly as God's servant. It could be that Jesus understood at least some of these texts as a further clue to the course of his own mission.

Numerous commentators affirm that Jesus regarded his suffering and death as requisite to the coming of the Kingdom of God.[56] Yet these writers are vague regarding the precise connection which Jesus was supposed to have seen between his prospective death and the advent of the Kingdom. Reference to Moses' procedure in ratifying the covenant (Exod. 24:3–8) or the "suffering servant" hymn (Isa. 52:13—53:12) does not alone explain the connec-

56. E.g., Rudolf Schnackenburg, *God's Rule and the Kingdom* (New York: Herder & Herder, 1963), pp. 192, 250–51; John A. T. Robinson, *Jesus and His Coming* (Nashville: Abingdon, 1957), p. 81.

tion,[57] nor do the later Christian atonement theories. If the passion predictions are not secondary, and if Jesus did regard his death as a matter of necessity, it was a matter of scriptural necessity (Mark 9:12; 14:21). The Scripture which Jesus himself cites, according to Mark 14:27, is Zech. 13:7. If Jesus understood this in connection with the prophecy in Zech. 3:8–10, which speaks of the removal of "the guilt of this land in a single day" and the subsequent coming of the Messiah and the Messianic Age, the blows which he would receive (and perhaps also his death) would "remove the guilt" vicariously, and thereby enable the Messianic Age to appear (Zech. 3:10). God would not establish His Kingdom in a guilty land.

The phrase "blood of the covenant" (Zech. 9:11) could then have informed his understanding of the special meaning of the wine (Mark 14:24). As the wine represented the coming Messianic Banquet, so, by analogy, it represented also his own blood, by which the final obstacle to the coming of the Kingdom would be removed—the guilt of the land (cf. Zech. 12:10—13:1). In Matt. 26:28, Jesus speaks of the cup as his "blood of the covenant . . . poured out for many [cf. Isa. 53:11b] for the forgiveness of sins." The forgiveness of sins is also seen as a requisite to entrance into the Kingdom, and perhaps also for its coming, in the "Lord's Prayer"; there, especially in the Lukan version (11:2–4), forgiveness of sins may have been understood as the way by which God might spare the faithful from temptation (peirasmos). Their guilt might yet be overcome by God's forgiveness. Or it may be that Schweitzer is correct in proposing that Jesus shared the belief of those Jewish apocalyptists who held that the Messianic Age could come only after the period of final tribulation (peirasmos), as indicated, for example, in Matt. 6:13, and Mark 14:38 and parallels.[58] In that case, Jesus would bear these tribulations on behalf of the people, sparing them the necessity of undergoing these pains and enabling the Kingdom at last to come. These theories are not mutually exclusive. In both cases Jesus would have visualized a scriptural and dogmatic connection between his suffering (and perhaps death) and the coming of the Kingdom of God. This connec-

---

57. Neither passage refers to the Messiah or the Kingdom of God. But Paul's characterization of the leaders of the Jerusalem Church as "pillars" (Gal. 2:9) may be based upon the Exodus text (24:4).

58. See also Dan. 7:21–27; 12:1 f.; Syr. Baruch 70.

tion may be indicated in Jesus' words which in some way or other were intended to suggest an analogy between the bread and his body, the wine and his blood (Mark 14:22–24). Possibly this also is implicit in his prayer that he might be spared the necessity of "this cup" (14:36), his own special act of preparation for the coming of the Kingdom of God, and perhaps also his own Messiahship.[59]

The early Church continued to re-enact the Last Supper of Jesus with his disciples in the hope that somehow doing so would constitute preparation for his return as Messiah and the beginning of the Messianic Age (I Cor. 11:26). It is not unlikely that the "Lord's Prayer" had its *Sitz im Leben* (though not its origin) in the early Church's daily or weekly celebrations of the Eucharist, the bread of the Eucharist representing the "bread for tomorrow," the messianic meal. The hope and prayer for the coming of the Kingdom later was given a specifically messianic or christological form: *marana tha*, "Our Lord, Come!" (*Didache* 10:1–6; cf. I Cor. 16:22; Rev. 22:20). Perhaps the early Christians expected that Jesus would return to them, and the Messianic Age begin, at one of these observances.[60] Luke and John may evidence this expectation in their report that the risen Jesus was revealed to his disciples "in the breaking of bread" (Luke 24:30–35; John 21:12 f.). In both instances, as at the banquet in the wilderness, they eat fish as well as bread.

The "breaking bread and the prayers" (Acts 2:42) practiced by the early Jerusalem Christians "day by day" (2:46) was evidently in anticipation of and preparation for the coming of the Kingdom.

59. Pannenberg states the matter of Jesus' understanding of the necessity of his death quite plausibly: "It would be very peculiar if Jesus had not reckoned at least with the possibility of his death in Jerusalem, though not in the sense of the predictions of the passion in the Gospels. . . . Nevertheless, his journey to Jerusalem was certainly no deed of despair. Jesus probably expected that God would, in one way or another, acknowledge him, even in the case of his own failure. This assumption is all the less to be rejected, since Jesus in any case reckoned with the imminent end of the world and the resurrection of the dead and judgment of the Son of Man which were associated with that. Measured by the imminent nearness of these events of the end, it must have been of secondary significance for Jesus whether he himself would have to endure death before the end came. The truth of his proclamation did not need to depend on this. One way or the other the ultimate confirmation of his message through the imminent fulfillment of all history with the appearance of the Son of Man on the clouds of heaven was immediately at hand" (*Jesus—God and Man*, pp. 65–66).

60. So Schweitzer, *Kingdom of God*, pp. 148–53.

The prayers presumably were for the coming of the Kingdom of God and of Jesus as Messiah (cf. Acts 3:19–21). The daily breaking of bread would have had the same meaning. Each day they hoped and prayed that the Kingdom would come "today."

Perhaps it was understood also that those who shared the food were marked out as heirs of the messianic banquet soon to commence when the Kingdom of God was established (cf. Acts 2:38–40; *Didache* 9:4). It was, indeed, a "Eucharist," a "thanksgiving" for the era of salvation that was coming. It seems unlikely that the early Church invented this association of the meal with the coming of the Kingdom of God. Instead, it is probable that their understanding was the same as that of Jesus and his companions at the Last Supper.

The later interpretation of the Eucharist as the "medicine of immortality" (John 6:48–58; Ignatius to *Ephesians* 20:2) continued to express the central connection between the meal and salvation, even though the latter is here "demythologized" in accordance with the tendency of the church to think of immortality and "heavenly mansions" (John 14:2 f.) instead of the coming of God's Kingdom on earth.

25. Jesus' Prayer at Gethsemane (Mark 14:32–40)

Synoptic tradition reports various occasions in which Jesus instructs his followers about prayer. Generally, he urges them to pray for the coming of the Kingdom of God. Prayer, implicitly, can move God to bring the Kingdom. It also represents the state of mind of those who trust God and are concerned to be ready for the Kingdom when it comes (Matt. 6:9–13=Luke 11:2–4; Luke 18:1–8). In Gethsemane he urges his three companions to "watch" (cf. Mark 13:33, 35–37 and parallels) and pray that they do not "enter into temptation" (*peirasmos*). The import of this admonition is the same as in the "Lord's Prayer": they are to pray that the Kingdom of God might come without their having to undergo the final tribulation or birth pangs of the Messianic Age. The Fourth Gospel reports that here Jesus himself prayed that God would "keep them from the Evil One," the one who would inflict the final *peirasmos* (John 17:15; cf. Matt. 6:13).

Jesus' own prayer apparently is to the same effect, that God, with whom all things are possible, might eliminate the necessity of his experiencing the final tribulation (Mark 14:35 f., 39). This means that God might bring the Kingdom, which he had assured his disciples He would indeed bring soon, without first permitting the otherwise requisite tribulation to ensue. Jesus evidently expected his companions to join him in this prayer (Mark 14:37 f.), a prayer, in effect, very much like that which he had previously given them as the essence of the matter (Matt. 6:10–13). Jesus himself had prayed on one or two occasions for the coming of the Kingdom without referring to the tribulation (Mark 11:14; cf. 14: 25).

In contemporary Jewish apocalyptic thought, the tribulation or birth pangs of the Messianic Age would be experienced by all of those who were on the earth at the time. It was not a special fate reserved for the Messiah or messiah-to-be.[61] Those who kept the faith, who endured to the end, however, would be "saved," i.e., granted entrance to the Coming age (cf. Dan. 12:1; Mark 13:13). It is not clear from the tradition about Jesus' prayer whether he visualized a special fate for himself, or whether he prayed that he, together with his followers, might be spared the tribulation which otherwise they would all have to share. He was willing to accept the tribulation himself, for, unless some special miracle of God's omnipotence and grace occurred, the Kingdom of God could not come. The divinely inspired prophetic (or apocalyptic) scriptures had decreed first tribulation, then Kingdom of God. But Jesus prayed that God might yet perform just this miracle and overrule the previous plan (cf. John 12:27). Jesus had no desire to suffer the tribulation, but if it were God's will that he do so in order that the Kingdom might come, he would go through with it.

26.   THE SAYING TO THE HIGH PRIEST AND SANHEDRIN
(MARK 14:62)

If we know anything about Jesus, it is that he was executed by the Romans as a pretender to the Jewish throne. Before he could be delivered over to the Roman authorities, it was necessary for his

61. Moore, *Judaism*, 2:361 f.

Jewish opponents to produce some kind of evidence. Jesus had not at any time claimed publicly to be the Messiah, perhaps because he did not feel that he was as yet entitled to that office.[62] Yet his behavior—especially his entrance into the city and his attempted purification of the Temple, and perhaps also his claim that he would rebuild it—had apparently led the Jewish authorities to suspect that he might have such ambitions, or, what was equally dangerous, that Roman authorities might think he did.[63] Yet he had not said that he was the King. How could they get "hard" evidence? Significantly, no witnesses could be found who could or would testify to this effect. So the High Priest came to the point and asked Jesus directly, "Are you the Christ?"[64] Perhaps he had been "tipped off" by Judas, as Schweitzer suggests. Or, perhaps he and the other Jewish authorities had simply drawn their own conclusions.

Only in the Markan version does Jesus answer unambiguously, "I am," and even here, immediately afterward, he speaks of the future manifestation of the Son of man as someone other than himself. Whether Jesus here acknowledged the title "Messiah" (cf. Mark 15:2), and whether he identified himself with the eschatological Son of man or not, his reference to the prospective appearance of the Son of man indicates that he expected his mission and message to be vindicated in the near future. The High Priest and his other accusers would "see the Son of man sitting at the right hand of God."[65] Perhaps Jesus meant that he himself would soon be revealed to them as the eschatological Son of man. At any rate, this promise—or warning—was not, in fact, fulfilled. It is improbable that the church would have invented such a saying.[66] Luke, who elsewhere readjusts the earlier tradition in order to show that Jesus did not expect the imminent arrival of the King-

62. It is not impossible that Bultmann is correct in maintaining that Jesus looked for someone else to come as Messiah. However, synoptic tradition as reviewed in the preceding chapters seems to indicate that Jesus understood himself to be the one who would soon be revealed as Messiah or, at any rate, Son of man. Or he may have thought that he was already the Messiah.

63. Luke 19:38; Mark 11:17; Mark 14:58. See Smith, *Paradox*, pp. 164–65.

64. The expression "the Son of the Blessed" is a circumlocution for "Son of God," an equivalent messianic title.

65. "Power," like "Blessed" (v. 61), is a Jewish circumlocution for the divine name.

66. Thus also Rudolf Otto, *The Kingdom of God and the Son of Man* (London: Lutterworth Press, 1938), p. 227; cf. Grässer, who thinks that it implies a delay of the parousia. Cf. J. A. T. Robinson, *Jesus*, p. 49.

dom, apparently changes the reading. The High Priest and Council did not live to see the eschatological Son of man; but—so reads Luke—Jesus did not say that they would, only that the Son of man would henceforth be seated at the right hand of God (Luke 22:69).[67] The Markan reading, repeated by Matthew, is evidently the earlier.

But even the Lukan version does not refer to Jesus' impending death. The expression "from now on" (*apo tou nun*), like Matthew's "hereafter" (*ap' arti*), means "henceforth," "from this moment afterward," and indicates that little or no time will elapse between these words and Jesus' vindication as or by the Son of man. It seems likely that a Q saying underlies both the Matthean and Lukan expressions. "From now on" in Luke contradicts not only the subsequent account of Jesus' execution and burial, but also the special Lukan tradition of his ascension after forty days (Acts 1:3–11). In both Matthew and Luke, it conflicts with the reports of Jesus' post-resurrection appearances among the disciples. Precisely because of these contradictions or conflicts, the prospect of imminent vindication would seem to have been the earlier idea. It was not fulfilled.

There are other evidences that Jesus expected immediate vindication through the dawning of the Messianic Age. According to Luke 23:42 f., Jesus assured the "thief" who believed him to be Messiah that "today" (*semeron*, cf. Matt. 6:11) they would both be in Paradise (sc. Kingdom, v. 42). This may reflect the idea which otherwise appears in the gospels only in Luke, that upon death one enters his ultimate abode immediately (cf. Luke 16:9, 19–31), as well as Luke's special concern for the *am-ha aretz*, so the authenticity of the saying is not beyond question. But the words as presented do not exclude the possibility of vindication before death.

Perhaps Jesus had hoped for deliverance from the gathering storm of opposition. He prayed for such deliverance (Mark 14:35–39). Scripture may have encouraged him to hope that he would live to see his vindication (Ps. 118:17; Isa. 53:10–12). Had he not instructed his followers to buy swords (Luke 22:36)? How could two swords be enough (22:38) unless God or His angels were also going to intervene? One of Jesus' disciples drew a sword (one of those acquired in accordance with Jesus' command?) and struck

67. Thus Bartsch, " 'Verfluchung,' " pp. 258–59.

the slave of the High Priest. How could any of this have to do with fulfilling Scripture (Luke 22:37; Mark 14:49b)? In Zech. 11:17 and 13:7, "the sword" was to strike the worthless shepherd, then God himself would intervene on behalf of his people (Zech. 13:7— 14:5). Do the various synoptic traditions about a sword or swords echo, if in garbled form, some saying of Jesus and some activity on the part of his disciples? Had not Jesus said that he came to bring a sword?[68] But the mob organized by the Jewish officials had more weapons than Jesus' followers and outnumbered them (Mark 14: 43, 48), and no legions of angels came to the rescue (Matt. 26:53).

Neither did Elijah, a swordsman of some repute (I Kings 19:1). Was it only in the imagination of the bystanders that Jesus called on Elijah (Mark 15:35 f.)? It is not impossible that his words were recast by the church to conform to the more acceptable utterance of Ps. 22:1. Or perhaps Jesus did begin to recite that psalm. In either case, Jesus' outcry or prayer (Mark 15:34) expressed his disappointment that God's deliverance had not yet come, and also, perhaps, his last hope that it still might do so before he died.

If at his trial Jesus was already reconciled to the necessity of his death as a prerequisite to the coming of the Kingdom, he expected that the priests and others before whom he stood would themselves soon be on trial before the Son of man. If he thought that he must first die, he also would have expected to be raised from the dead, for like the Pharisees he believed in the resurrection. It would take place at the beginning of the Coming age. Perhaps it was to be through death and resurrection that he would be transformed into the messianic Son of man.[69] Or perhaps God would vindicate him, show him to be the Messiah, and bring His Kingdom first. In either case, the High Priest and his fellow-accusers would soon be in for the surprise of their lives![70] With the coming of the Son of man, Jesus' accusers would join the ranks of the accused.

68. Matt. 10:34; cf. Luke 12:49 ff. Thus also Betz, "Heiliger Krieg," pp. 128 ff.

69. Cf. Isa. 53:8–12. See Schweitzer, *Kingdom of God*, pp. 103–7, and secs. 4 and 8 of this study.

70. Cf. Cranfield, *St. Mark*, p. 444: "If then the reference in *opsesthe* [14:62] is to the Parousia, is it implied that the Parousia is expected to occur during the lifetime of the High Priest and his associates? Surely not!" Cranfield does not wish Jesus or the church to have been mistaken about the delay of the parousia (p. 408). But on p. 445 he admits that Jesus might have meant that he would come as Judge "during their lifetimes"!

V

Subsequently and Consequently

THAT Jesus expected the Kingdom of God to come in the near future cannot be disputed by anyone who takes the synoptic evidence seriously. This expectation is also evidenced in the initially urgent and even later continuing expectation on the part of the early Church. But the fact that the Kingdom of God did not come posed a problem for the Church. The hope for the coming of the Kingdom, and the fact that it has not come, also are matters of theological interest and significance in the contemporary situation.

27. THE EXPECTATIONS OF THE EARLY CHURCH

It is questionable whether Jesus had really prepared his followers for his death. From the time of his arrest through the various reported resurrection appearances, they seem to have been under a spell of continual fear and confusion. That Jesus had died was, of course, a scandal to Christians as well as to "Jews."[1] Contrary to a certain popularization of the Dead Sea Scrolls, no known Jewish tradition from the period betrays any expectation that the Messiah was to die. The earliest Christians were preoccupied with the effort to understand and explain it by reference to Scripture or theological argument (e.g., Luke 24; Romans 3:21—11:36). It may well be that the passion predictions and other traditions indicative of Jesus' anticipation of his death, together with a growing collection of scriptural "prophecies" purporting to account for it, all originated in the Church as Jesus' followers attempted to comprehend the fact and meaning of his death.

1. I Cor. 1:23. All of the earliest Christians also were Jews.

106

But if Jesus saw anything in his death, it was in one way or another related to the coming of the Kingdom of God. Certain traditions indicate that the early Christians also saw some such connection. The peculiar eschatological phenomena reported at the time of Jesus' expiration suggest that there were some who thought that such things should have occurred at this time (Matt. 27:45, 51–54; Luke 23:44 f.).[2] Mark reports that on the day of Jesus' death, shortly afterward, a certain Joseph of Arimathea was "eagerly expecting" (*prosdechomenos*) the Kingdom to come (15:43).

Instead of returning to Galilee, at least some of Jesus' followers remained in Jerusalem, "breaking bread" and praying, evidently expecting something decisive to happen. Acts 1:6 indicates what this was: they were expecting the restoration of the Kingdom to Israel. Curiously, especially for a Lukan tradition, Jesus does not correct the political overtones of this expectation, but tells them that it was not for them "to know times or seasons" (1:7). Luke implies, though, that Jesus himself knew or knows. Here we see a tradition which serves both to explain the fact that, in Luke's time, the Kingdom, "the appointed time," had not yet come, and to demonstrate that Jesus himself had been fully aware that it was not yet about to come (cf. Luke 19:11). It is further suggested (1:8) that the final time will not come until the Gospel has been preached "to the end of the earth," i.e., to all the Gentiles or nations. These traditions suggest that the historical Jesus had given his followers some reason to expect that the Kingdom would come, in Jerusalem, upon his death. Where else should the Messiah be revealed and enthroned? He had earlier expected or hoped that the Kingdom might come without his having to die. Possibly he hoped to the very last that it might do so. Perhaps his followers still hoped that it would come despite his death. The reports and visions of his reappearance from the dead must have given credence to this hope, for the resurrection was to take place at the beginning of the New age. The resurrection of Jesus would have been at least a good omen for the hope that the other eschatological promises would soon be fulfilled.[3] In the meantime, it was understood that

2. So also Werner, *Formation*, p. 33, and J. Grassi, "Ezekiel xxxvii, 1–14 and the New Testament," *NTS* 11 (1965):162–64.

3. Thus also Hans-Werner Bartsch, "Early Christian Eschatology," *NTS* 11 (1965):392–97. Pannenberg has recently made clear this relationship: "The significance of Jesus' resurrection was originally bound to the fact that it constituted only the beginning of the universal resurrection of the dead and the

after his death Jesus was raised to the messianic office in heaven
(Rom. 1:3 f.; Acts 2:36). Thus Jesus of Nazareth had been transformed into the supernatural Christ. It still remained for him to
come to earth as the Christ.[4]

The saying attributed to the risen Jesus in Acts 1:6–8 is of a piece
with synoptic apocalyptic thought: the "end" would not take place
until the Gospel had been preached to the Gentiles.[5] All of the
synoptic evangelists still expected that the Kingdom of God would
come soon, but it had not come at the time they were writing.
Earlier, Paul had been confident that it would come in the course
of his own lifetime (I Thess. 4:15–17; I Cor. 15:51 f.).

In early times the Church celebrated the Lord's Supper with the
expectation that the Lord (Jesus, now the Christ) himself would
reappear in this setting. Christians prayed for the coming of Jesus
as the Christ from the time of Paul into the second century.[6] Some
of Jesus' contemporaries began to die, including the High Priest
and members of the Council who were supposed to witness his
vindication. Sayings such as Mark 9:1 f. ("Some standing here . . .")
and 13:30 ("This generation will not [sc., entirely] pass away until
. . .") were probably shaped during this period.[7] Finally, the last
of Jesus' (supposed) companions, "the beloved disciple," died, contrary to the general expectation that this one, at least, would live
to see the coming of the Messiah and Kingdom (John 21:20–23).
The irritation evident in the response attributed to Jesus here and

---

end of the world" (*Jesus—God and Man*, p. 106). Pannenberg's position is
that the fact that Jesus and the early Church erred in expecting the Kingdom to come in their own generation (pp. 106, 226) does not refute the
Christian faith. Rather, Jesus' resurrection validates Christian hope for the ultimate fulfillment of the end events (pp. 107–8, 226, 242–43).

4. See Werner, *Formation*, pp. 126–29; cf. Robinson, *Twelve New Testament Studies*, pp. 139–53.

5. Mark 13:10; Matt. 24:14; cf. Matt. 28:19 f.; Luke 21:24; 24:47.

6. I Cor. 16:22; Rev. 22:20, cf. 22:7; *Didache* 10:6.

7. Thus also Grässer, *Das Problem*, pp. 128–37, 177–78. Cf. A. L. Moore,
The Parousia in the New Testament, Supplements to *Novum Testamentum*,
vol. 13 (Leiden: Brill, 1966). Moore argues that these sayings are authentic,
but that Jesus' expectation of the parousia was not "delimited"; thus, Jesus
was not in error. Consequently, for the modern interpreter, there can be "no
question of abandoning an outmoded hope" (pp. 191, 207). Moore's otherwise valuable study is vitiated by this dogmatic interest, which is also reflected
in his assumption as "axiomatic" that the Kingdom of God and the person (or
"person and work") of Jesus are "inseparable." His citation of Origen's *autobasileia* concept as authority is not reassuring (p. 104). Origen's interests
were scarcely historical!

in subsequent responses to "scoffers" indicates the anxiety of those who were beginning to experience some doubt whether it would come in their lifetimes.[8]

As time went on, various further explanations were offered for the delay. The Fourth Gospel represents, though not as perfectly or consistently as the Bultmann school supposes, a tendency toward the elimination or demythologizing of the eschatological expectations. Eternal life, starting on earth, to be completed in heaven, begins to replace the longing for the coming of the Kingdom of God on earth. Jesus will not need to come as Messiah (though his coming for final redemption is still anticipated),[9] for he had already come as such. Similarly, Judgment has at least begun in the responses of men to Jesus, the only Son of God, the light (John 3:16–21). Another solution was the proposal that the delay was granted to permit a greater number to repent (II Pet. 3:9). Accompanying this is the proposal that, with God, time is measured on a different scale (II Pet. 3:8), but this is not seen as a literal millenialism: the "day of the Lord" still might come at any time (II Pet. 3:10–14; I Clem. 23:4–5).

Throughout the New Testament period, Christians continued to live in this eschatological context, convinced, yet also reminding one another that "the end of all things is at hand" (I Pet. 4:7); that "it is the last hour" (I John 2:18, 28); that "the coming of the Lord is at hand . . . the Judge is standing at the doors" (James 5:8 f.); "For yet a little while, and the Coming one shall come and shall not tarry" (Heb. 10:37).

As late as the fourth century, those who framed the "Nicene" creed still affirmed their hope that they would have a share in "the life of the world to come." And to the present time, though scarcely comprehending its eschatological meaning, Christians continue to repeat the prayer "Thy Kingdom come. . . ."

28.   THE HISTORICAL, ESCHATOLOGICAL JESUS

Less can be known about the historical Jesus than is supposed by those who regard the Gospels as objective, reliable records. None

---

8. *I Clem.* 23:3; II Pet. 3:3 ff.; Jude 17 ff.; *II Clem.* 11:2 f.
9. John 14:3, 21 ff. Cf. II Tim. 4:1, 8, 18.

of them was written by any of Jesus' companions; all are dependent upon earlier tradition, much of which had been reshaped or even produced in accordance with the situations and beliefs of the emerging Christian communities. These had come to regard Jesus as the Messiah, and, by virtue of his resurrection, as a supernatural being. It is natural that something of these qualities was projected into their recollection and retelling of his historical career (e.g., Mark 6:47–52; 9:2–8).[10] The stories of Jesus' birth (Matt. 1–2; Luke 1–2; 3:23–38) reflect this tendency, which is epitomized in the omniscient and omnipotent divine Christ portrayed in the Fourth Gospel.

There are no "laws" or absolute criteria for distinguishing between traditions that actually go back to Jesus and those which arose or were altered significantly in the early Christian communities. But where divergent or conflicting accounts or ideas appear, one may often determine which is likely to be the earlier. For instance, where one version "corrects" the theological viewpoint of another in order to conform to the Church's beliefs, the uncorrected version is probably earlier (e.g., Mark 10:17; cf. Matt. 19:16). Or where a tradition appears which seems to have been intended to explain why an earlier expectation was not actualized, it is more plausible that the explanation is secondary than that the expectation was (e.g., Luke 19:11; John 21:23). In this connection, an aura of authenticity attaches to prophetic utterances which were not fulfilled (e.g., Matt. 10:23; Mark 13:2; 14:62). Why should the church have invented such sayings? Similarly, reports purporting to show that certain expectations were fulfilled, typically by a miracle of some sort but not in the sense evidently intended by Jesus, are likely to be secondary (e.g., Mark 6:42 f.; 11:20 f.; cf. Matt. 21:19c–20; 27:51–53).

Reports of sayings or actions of Jesus which show a pattern of internal coherence are more likely to be authentic than isolated sayings or episodes which evidence contradictory purpose or understanding. Likewise, traditions which are "difficult" or incomprehensible to the evangelists (e.g., the "sign of Jonah" saying or the prayer about not eating figs) are likely to be more authentic than their "explanations." Authentic material may also be found where the viewpoint of Jesus or his companions appears incidentally, without coming to the attention of the evangelist as a problem

10. See Smith, *Paradox*, pp. 16 ff.

(e.g., Mark 10:40). Other criteria and considerations might be enumerated. The point of interest here, however, is that the pattern of internal coherence appearing in a great deal of tradition, which generally seems earlier rather than later, discloses a Jesus who spoke and acted consistently with the belief that the Kingdom of God would soon be established on earth.

It is possible, of course, that the traditions which are consistent with this pattern were all invented by the early Church. For reasons of their own, some early Christians might have wished to create the impression that Jesus and his companions had looked for an early actualization of the Kingdom of God. Later Christians might then have attempted to correct the erroneous record left by the earlier custodians of the tradition in the light of their awareness that the Kingdom had not come. It is possible that the eschatological Jesus was a literary fiction produced by the earliest Christian community. But it is more probable that the eschatological Jesus was the historical Jesus.

This is not to say, of course, that every eschatological feature attributed to him in the Gospels or in interpretations of Gospel tradition must be regarded as authentic. Many of the suggestions and questions raised in this study are presented only as possibilities. Further investigation may add to or diminish the likelihood of certain proposals. In many instances, there will probably never be enough evidence to justify more than conjecture. Nevertheless, though many of the particular suggestions sketched here are problematic, the basic pattern seems to be established. More can be known about the historical Jesus than is supposed by those who ignore or deny the eschatological nature of his ministry.

The outlook and purpose of Jesus is to be seen not only in his words but also in his activity. In Galilee, Jesus proclaimed that the Kingdom of God was near and that men should repent. Elijah had come, the Spirit of prophecy had been restored. Men were living now in the last days of the Old world. Jesus undertook to exorcise demons in order to liberate the afflicted from the power of the Evil One, preparing them for entrance into the Kingdom, and to prepare for the final defeat of Satan which would take place, if not earlier, then with the establishment of God's rule on earth. The defeat of the demons was a sure sign of Satan's ultimate doom. At moments, perhaps, Jesus even visualized the defeat of Satan and the coming of the Kingdom as if they were already present realities. He sent his followers to hasten through the towns of "Israel" in order to extend his work of preparation for the Kingdom, convinced that it would come in the next few weeks. Should his fellow Jews still be in Satan's grip or unrepentant at the dawn of the Messianic Age, it would not be well for them. The Twelve returned, followed by a great crowd aroused by their preaching and, perhaps, by their successful exorcisms. Jesus consecrated this believing and hopeful crowd as heirs to the Kingdom by a symbolic pre-enactment of the Messianic Banquet. Perhaps he hoped that God might then inaugurate the Kingdom, there in the Galilean wilderness (cf. Isa. 40:3–5). But the Kingdom did not come.

Jesus proceeded to Jerusalem to complete his work of preparing for the Kingdom, confident that it would be manifested there. There he would be enthroned as King to preside at the Judgment, joined in this work, perhaps, by some or all of his disciples. Possibly he expected the Kingdom to dawn with his entrance into the city. He prayed that it would, at any rate, come within the next few weeks, before it is the season for figs. The days before Passover he spent in the Temple, purifying it in accordance with prophetic traditions, preparing it for the beginning of the Messianic Age, and teaching those who would hear about the imminence of the Kingdom. He ate the Passover meal with his disciples in Jerusalem, hoping perhaps that the Kingdom might come that evening or the next day—at any rate, before the next Passover. Still it did not come. Possibly he and his friends would have to suffer or even die before it could come, for it was written that tribulation must precede the Messianic Age. But he taught his followers to pray, and prayed himself, that they might be spared the tribulation. At his trial and on the cross, he still looked for the Kingdom to come, either before or in consequence of his death. It did not come, but later some of his followers thought that with and through his death and resurrection, certain features of the Coming age had been manifested. Now they could look for Jesus to come as Messiah or Son of man, and for the coming of the Kingdom of God at any time. He did not come. It did not come.

Jews, Christians, and others from the first century to the present time have tried to find some category into which Jesus could be placed. To Jews, he was a rabbi or teacher, albeit somewhat misguided. To Christians, he became the Son of God, no longer a messianic category but a "person" of the Trinity, having two natures, divine and human. To Muslims he was a prophet. In modern times, he has been explained as a political reformer, messianic plotter, and existentialist.[11] In common, these explanations discount or ignore the eschatological character of Jesus' outlook and actions.

Not all of Jesus' ideas and activities derived from his eschatological beliefs. His conception of God's righteousness and mercy were grounded in the Scriptures and in traditional Jewish piety, informed by his own religious awareness. His understanding of nature and human nature, while related to his belief in God, was also based on his own observations, especially his perception of the human capacity for pretension and self-serving (e.g., Luke 16: 1–8; 18:10–12) as well as for faith and love (e.g., Mark 12:41–44; Luke 10:29–37). But for Jesus, these understandings were bound up with his expectation that God was about to establish his Kingdom on earth. Then the righteousness and mercy of God would be manifested in the exclusion of the impenitent and unrighteous from its blessings, and the inclusion of the "meek," the poor, and the loving. The historical Jesus was not quite same as the Jesus of either traditional or liberal Christianity.

He was more dogmatic than liberal Christianity wished to admit, though his dogmas were more like those of apocalyptic Judaism than orthodox Christian theology. Contrary to liberal theology, he may well have "given himself," or at any rate willingly accepted the prospect of suffering and death, in order to mediate the redemption of the world. But the "redemption" he contemplated was the coming of the eschatological Kingdom of God to earth, not the pietistic or sacramental saving of souls for a spiritual, eternal life somewhere else. Contrary to the canons of orthodox theology, he did not regard himself as an omniscient and omnipotent divine being. He may have thought of himself as Messiah or the one who would be enthroned as Messiah when the Coming age was revealed. But he was mistaken in his hope that the Kingdom would soon come. It has not come yet.

The task in this study is mainly historical rather than theological. The interest is in attempting to describe the intention of the historical Jesus as evidenced in the actions and words attributed to him in the available documents.[12] The eschatological character of

11. E.g., S. G. F. Brandon, Hugh J. Schonfield. See Schweitzer, *Psychiatric Study*, and chaps. 1 and 3 of Hiers, *Jesus and Ethics*.
12. It goes without saying that the synoptic evangelists were not interested

the historical Jesus does suggest certain theological implications, however.

It suggests that the initial differences between Christians and Jews may not be as great as indicated in later elaborations, especially of Christian theology. Jesus looked for the coming of the Kingdom of God or Messianic Age, and may have expected to become the Messiah. Early Christians also looked for the coming of the Messianic Age, and believed that it was Jesus who would come as Messiah. Traditional Judaism, if less apocalyptic than in the first century, continues to look for the coming of the Messiah and Messianic Age. The decisive difference has to do with the identity of the coming Messiah: Jesus of Nazareth, or another? In both cases, it was expected that God will bring the Kingdom.

It is not likely that many people in the twentieth century, Jews, Christians, or others, will be willing or able to adopt as their own the world view or "mythology" of the first century of the common era. But it should be possible to ask what basic affirmations about God, man, and the world are expressed in these "myths," once literally held but now no longer tenable as models for thinking about time and space. Here, at any rate, there is room for genuine ecumenical "dialogue" between and among Jews, Christians, and other modern men and women. There is no lack of interest at the present time in the question of the meaning of life in an eschatological context, whether in the case of Marxist or New Left hopes for "the Revolution" or even something beyond that, or uneasy bourgeois longings for a Kingdom of "Law and Order" or even "the Great Society." Existentialist and psychoanalytic schools combine and conflict in the quest for self-realization or authentic existence. Some seek an individualistic psychedelic paradise, a secular counterpart to the beatific vision. The quest for life in new worlds (e.g., Mars) goes on with a kind of sentimental religious hope that there, perhaps, a better life can be found, while in the old world (Earth), life comes and goes mixed with frustration and despair. Overall, quantum physicists and astronomers speculate as to the manner in which the earth, solar system, galaxy, and cosmos will be destroyed, if not also created anew.

Does the Christian tradition have anything to offer in helping

---

in writing "objective history." But it does not follow that their writings are useless as historical sources, even if their theological and other interests must be taken into account.

modern men understand the nature and meaning of existence and nonexistence in the midst of these hopes and fears? It may be that at least some of the perceptions and affirmations which underlie the eschatological beliefs of Judaism, Jesus, and the early church have a continuing vitality and relevance. Here the possibility, in fact the certainty, that historical existence on earth will come to an end is acknowledged without despair. The ambiguous character of historical existence is not taken as final, but there is no illusion that man is capable (by technology, behavioral or social engineering) of ultimately resolving these ambiguities into a life of individual or social perfection. Yet the value of life and being is not deprecated. The interim is an existence marked by moral seriousness, concern for the well-being of others, and the fulfillment of life rather than absurdity, egoism, and futility. Moral effort exerted against the flux of history does not lapse into passivity, cynical indifference, or hatred of the enemies of the movement when human and social realities fail to fall into the envisioned perfection. A higher Will or Purpose is affirmed than that of finite and pretentious men. Its actualizations are at best partial and transitory, yet this Purpose is trusted to bring about that which is ultimately good for the whole realm of being. Man does not redeem the cosmos; yet life is to be lived in the world, in affirming others and oneself in the milieus and processes of being, becoming, and extinction. Such motifs have been variously elaborated, in the writing of Teilhard de Chardin, A. N. Whitehead, H. R. Niebuhr, Paul Tillich. Our concern here is to indicate that the eschatological beliefs of Jesus and the early Church and of prophetic and apocalyptic Judaism need not be regarded simply as quaint myths. Neither are they to be taken literalistically as science or prophecy. The important theological problem is to find the meaning of the "myth."

The new "theology of hope," particularly as it may be seen in the continuing work of Wolfhart Pannenberg and Carl E. Braaten, represents a major effort in this direction. These theologians are not satisfied with Bultmann's existentialistic demythologizing which collapses past and future into a series of moments in the "now." The theologians of hope proceed both from a more accurate historical exegesis, which recognizes the fundamental significance of the future orientation for the biblical faith, and also from a more profound appreciation of the theological relevance of the future for the present human situation.

But is not the historical, *eschatological* Jesus too unlike the Christ of "the kerygma" or traditionalist Christian theology? If the historical, eschatological Jesus seems alien to our view, it is because we have grown accustomed to an unhistorical, uneschatological Jesus. Beginning as early as the composition of the gospels, and in the course of twenty centuries of developing doctrines, the churches have assigned to Jesus those characteristics that seemed best to express their understanding of who he was and is. Necessarily, the eschatological features of his message and mission have been, to a large extent, replaced and overlaid. But when this is recognized, would it not be an act of bad faith to continue to affirm that the (largely noneschatological) Jesus of the Fourth Gospel, or image of Christ in the mind of the ordinary churchman in the pew, and the historical Jesus are the same?[13]

The Christian claim that Jesus is the Christ can be neither validated nor invalidated by historical research. It would not prove that Jesus was the Messiah even if it could be demonstrated that he had supposed that he was or would be. The possible and probable results of historical criticism cannot take the place of the decisions of faith. Conversely, the claims of faith cannot preclude the findings of historical research. In the quest for the historical Jesus, fideism has been a greater obstacle to the truth than "historicism." Faith, of course, can proceed without reference to history. In that case, however, it cannot also claim to be grounded in history. Even the affirmation of "thatness" presupposes some understanding as to the content and meaning of "that" which is pointed to.[14]

Perhaps there was some connection between Jesus' intention or "understanding of the meaning of existence" and that expressed in the "kerygma" of the Church. If so, it is not likely to be discovered until the specifically eschatological features of Jesus' intention are taken at full value. Or it may be that the Church's interpretation(s) of Jesus' activity and significance bear little or no essential relation to Jesus' own intention or "self-understanding." Both the Christian

13. See, e.g., Martin Kähler, *The So-Called Historical Jesus and the Historic Biblical Christ,* 1892, 1896 (Philadelphia: Fortress, 1964), pp. 66 ff., 79 ff.
14. Contrary to R. Bultmann, "The Primitive Christian Kerygma and the Historical Jesus," in *The Historical Jesus and the Kerygmatic Christ,* eds. Carl E. Braaten and Roy A. Harrisville (Nashville: Abingdon, 1964), pp. 20 ff. See Keck's critique of Bultmann's dichotomy between faith and historical-critical research (*A Future,* pp. 54 f.).

and the scholar should be willing to take the risk of discovering the truth about the historical Jesus, whether congenial to any particular theology or philosophy or not.

At all events, if we wish to learn anything about the historical Jesus, we shall have to turn to the historical, eschatological Jesus. The sources do not tell us about any other historical Jesus.

Index of Primary Citations

119

OLD TESTAMENT APOCRYPHA AND PSEUDEPIGRAPHA

Post-Canonical

Index of Authors

Arndt, W. F., 75
Aune, D. E., 6, 91

Bartsch, H. W., 84, 104, 107
Bauer, W., 75
Betz, O., 5, 7, 50, 61, 87, 94, 105
Billerbeck, P., 48, 52, 60, 93
Blenkinsopp, J., 81
Boobyer, G. H., 67
Bornkamm, G., 1, 7, 60
Braaten, C. E., 115 f.
Brandon, S. G. F., 113
Bultmann, R., 1, 4 f., 11, 42, 56, 60, 88, 103, 116
Burrows, M., 5, 7

Cadbury, H. J., 5
Chardin, P. T. de, 115
Cranfield, C. E. B., 25, 34, 66, 91, 97, 105
Creed, J., 58

Davies, W. D., 54
Daube, W., 54
Deegan, D. L., 1
Dibelius, M., 5, 7
Dodd, C. H., 4 f., 60, 69
Doeve, J. W., 87

Enslin, M. S., 5 f., 15 f., 23, 82, 86, 91
Eppstein, V., 86
Evans, C. F., 72, 80

Fairhurst, A. M., 36
Farmer, W. R., 8
Filson, F. V., 72
Francis, F. O., 92
Freedman, D. N., 7
Fuller, R. H., 63

Gärtner, B., 94
Gingrich, F. W., 75
Ginsberg, L., 58
Goodenough, E. R., 69
Grant, R. M., 5, 7, 80
Grässer, E., 5, 73, 88, 103, 108
Grassi, J., 107
Grundmann, W., 54, 60

Hamilton, N. Q., 86 f.
Harnack, A. von, 4, 11
Harrisville, R. A., 116
Hengel, M., 10
Hiers, R. H., 3 f., 9, 12, 15 f., 19, 23, 29, 33, 40, 51, 54, 56, 66, 75, 82, 87, 113
Higgins, A. J. B., 96
Holland, D. L., 3, 12

Iersel, B. van, 67

Jeremias, J., 48, 50, 96 f.

Kähler, M., 116
Käsemann, E., 1 f.
Keck, L. E., 1, 6, 62, 116
Kee, H. C., 3, 60, 76
Kraeling, C. H., 55
Kuhn, H. W., 78

Manson, W., 26, 78
Minear, P. S., 52
Moore, A. L., 108
Moore, G. F., 54, 102

Niebuhr, H. R., 19, 115

Oesterly, W. O. E., 96
Otto, R., 103

UNIVERSITY OF FLORIDA MONOGRAPHS

Humanities

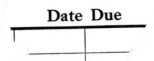

Date Due